D0984532

TOTAL QUALITY LIFE

STRATEGIES FOR PURPOSEFUL LIVING

STAN TOLER

wesleyan
publishing
house

Indianapolis, Indiana

Copyright © 2007 by Wesleyan Publishing House
Published by Wesleyan Publishing House
Indianapolis, Indiana 46250
Printed in the United States of America
ISBN: 978-0-89827-360-1

Library of Congress Cataloging-in-Publication Data

Toler, Stan.
  Total quality life : strategies for purposeful living / Stan Toler.
      p. cm.
  Includes bibliographical references.
  ISBN 978-0-89827-360-1
  1. Christian life. 2. Success--Religious aspects--Christianity. I.
Title.
  BV4501.3.T653 2007
  646.7--dc22

                            2007014314

This book contains advice and information relating to health and medicine. It is not intended to replace medical advice and should be used to supplement rather than replace regular care by your physician. Readers are encouraged to consult their physicians with specific questions and concerns.

The Web addresses (URLs) recommended throughout this book are solely offered as a resource to the reader. The citation of these Websites does not in any way imply an endorsement on the part of the author or the publisher, nor do the author or publisher vouch for their content for the life of this book.

CONTENTS

To my first grandson, Rhett Aaron Toler—
May you experience the same great quality of life that
I have enjoyed. In the words of your great uncle Terry Toler,
"May all your dreams come true!"

PREFACE

I f you are interested in achieving your personal best in every area of your life, this book is for you!

Whether it's a career that's gotten a bit off track, a checkbook that won't seem to balance, or those few extra pounds that refuse to go away, most of us have experienced the frustration and dissatisfaction that comes from realizing that the reality of our lives does not match the goal—our personal vision of a quality life.

Quality is a term we most often apply in the world of business, but total quality can describe your life as well—the complete fitness of your mind, body, resources, and spirit. When every area of life is in perfect harmony, and we are functioning with excellence and effectiveness, that is what I call *Total Quality Life*.

That won't happen by accident.

Most of us realize that achieving a life of balance and control will not come automatically, and it won't be easily achieved. It'll require a significant investment of time and energy, and it will require sacrifice. Yet the goal of total quality is worth the effort! I applaud you for your desire to make positive changes in your life, and offer you this word of encouragement as you begin: You can do it! You can become the person that you desire to be; you can live the Total Quality Life.

—STAN TOLER

ACKNOWLEDGMENTS

Special thanks to Don Cady, Lawrence Wilson, and the entire team at Wesleyan Publishing House for their vision and support for this project. I appreciate their partnership in making this book a reality.

Thanks also to Pat Diamond, Deloris Leonard, Mary McNeil, Jim Watkins, and Julie-Allyson Ieron for their expert assistance and advice.

Prerequisites
for
Total Quality

TQL never happens by accident.

To achieve it you must first have two essential items
that will guide you in your quest.

One is resolve, and the other is vision.

1

RESOLVE

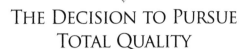

The Decision to Pursue Total Quality

The most difficult step in your quest for
total quality will be the first one.
You must choose the Total Quality Life.

Have you ever had one of those days? The alarm goes off way too early. You leap out of bed (eventually), throw on your gear, and head to the gym. Once on the treadmill, though, you hesitate when it asks you to enter a length of time for your workout. If you hadn't hit the snooze button twice, you could get in the forty-five minutes you promised yourself to make up for sleeping in yesterday. Now you have to weigh being late for work against keeping your commitment to exercise. You mentally run through your schedule and realize you don't have a meeting until nine. Even if you're late for work, you'll still have a half hour to prepare. Forty-five minutes it is.

Feeling virtuous, you hit *start* on the treadmill and *play* on your MP3, thinking you'll multitask by starting that audio book by the latest management guru. You realize, however, that you forgot to download it and are now stuck with your daughter's most recent (and somewhat disturbing) musical selections. At least they make you run faster, so you have a more vigorous workout. Back in the locker room, you can't remember the combination to your new lock. You have to wait for the custodian to find his bolt cutters and chop it off. Meanwhile, the clock's ticking, and you can't even shower. The maintenance guy finally shows up and makes a point of flexing a bit as he cuts the lock. You glance down at your own flabby abs and mutter, "Thanks."

> *The most difficult thing is the decision to act. The rest is tenacity.*
>
> —Robyn Davidson

After a quick shower, you jump into your car, steer toward the nearest Starbucks for your must-have Venti® vanilla *latte*, then rush to the office. Rounding the corner into the parking lot, your coffee sloshes the tiniest bit, but with deadly aim, and hits your shirt—right between the top two buttons. Your meeting starts in twenty minutes, so going home to change is out of the question. Now, the presentation that should have been a snap will be an ugly embarrassment.

After the meeting, you rush back to your office to check e-mail, but first you have to put out two department fires. It's after eleven when you finally boot up your computer. You have forty-seven new e-mails, and the voice mail light on your phone is flashing. You dig out from under the pile of messages and realize you've missed a conference call with a valued client.

Why does this keep happening to me? you wonder. You're trying so hard to be healthy, professional, and in control, but it doesn't seem to be working. What are you doing wrong?

Any of these minor mishaps could happen to anyone on a given day. In fact, this exact scenario happened to a friend of mine who works for a major corporation. We all have bad days now and then. Yet for many of us, days like this are not the exception. Try as we might, we always seem to be running a few minutes late, narrowly missing deadlines, and apologizing to someone for something. We envision a life of balance, composure, and control, but we experience a life marked by disorder, tension, and frustration. Is it possible to move from being engulfed by circumstances to being in control of our personal, professional, and spiritual lives?

Yes, it is possible to live with purpose, effectiveness, and significance. It's what I call TQL—Total Quality Life—and that life can be yours.

TOTAL QUALITY LIFE

Total Quality Life may seem like an unrealistic goal, but I assure you it is not. Achieving TQL is a process that takes, well, a lifetime, so it won't be easy. You'll need to persevere even when you're frustrated or tired. You'll need to choose wisely when you'd rather not choose at all. Most of all, you'll need a firm commitment to living up to your potential in each area of life. It is that commitment—that vision of a total quality life—that will help keep you going.

That's why the first step in experiencing TQL is a decision. It is not just a decision; it is *the* decision that underlies and supports all that follows. It is the decision that life in the future must be different than life in the present. It is the decision to change. That decision is fueled by a dissatisfaction with the disorder and frustration you currently experience. It is a decision to embrace a vision for a better life, a more balanced life, a total quality life.

Are you ready to make that decision? Are you ready to admit that changes must be made in your life? Before answering, you may want some idea of where your decision will lead. What will it mean to pursue a life of total quality? What will be involved?

FINDING A UNIQUE SOLUTION

A life of total quality will be a bit different for each of us because we are unique people. Even if you and I both need to manage our time at work better, I may need to spend less time on the phone, for example, and you may need to spend more. Rather than allowing an associate to unload all his personal problems onto me during a business call, I may need to get off the phone and finish those reports I've been procrastinating. But instead of reading a professional journal, you may need to pick up the phone and reestablish communication with a valued customer. Likewise, even if Jack and Jill both need to improve their diets, Jack may need to eat more fruits and vegetables while Jill may need more protein.

So your TQL will look different from mine—and that's fine. The principles I'll share in this book are meant to be individualized and customized. Every day brings new opportunities to do just that.

HARNESSING THE POWER OF CHOICE

Along with opportunities, each day brings many choices. Some are major and some are minor; some deal with our personal

Gutsy Determination: Eric Liddell

In the 1924 Olympic Games in Paris, star runner Eric Liddell had a difficult decision to make. He was scheduled to run his best event, the 100 meters, on a Sunday. But as a devout Christian, Liddell objected to competing on Sunday. He determined to remain true to his principles even if it meant forfeiting the chance to win.

At the last moment, teammate Harold Abrams switched events with Liddell. Liddell ran the 400 on Tuesday and Abrams, who was Jewish, ran the 100 on Sunday. Both men honored their faiths (Abram celebrated the Jewish Sabbath on Saturday). And both men won—even though not running in their best events. Abrams won gold. Liddell also came in first while breaking the world record for the 400 meters.

Liddell lived a quality life by putting God first in everything he did, eventually dying in a Chinese concentration camp during WWII.

lives and some with our work; some are responses to opportunity while others are forced upon us by negative circumstances.

While it may seem there really are no good choices available in some cases—such as when you feel stuck in a job that offers little potential for advancement or when communication has broken down between you and your spouse—in reality, we always have the power to choose two things: our attitude and our behavior. By using the power of choice, we can change *any* negative pattern that disrupts the total quality of our lives. And by changing our own negative patterns, we can change a great many of the circumstances that swirl around us.

We can choose TQL, even when it seems we are locked into unfortunate circumstances. (We'll discuss more about how to harness that power in future chapters.)

GAINING CONTROL IN ALL AREAS

Each one of us is a complete person—a whole person. Yet at times it seems our lives are fractured into several parts. Things may be going reasonably well at work; but if there are problems in your personal life, your career suffers, too. In the same way, if you are not on top physically, health problems may cause difficulty in your relationships or finances.

Experiencing TQL involves gaining balance and control in four critical areas of life: thought life, physical well-being, assets and resources, and spirituality. To put it another way, TQL happens when you gain control of your mind, body, money, and spirit. When these areas are disjointed or disconnected, you will experience chaos. When they are ordered and aligned, you will have a total quality life.

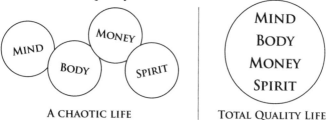

A CHAOTIC LIFE | TOTAL QUALITY LIFE

We'll explore each of these areas in Part Two of this book. For now, understand that the quality of your life is directly related to how you nourish, maintain, and grow all four of these areas. If you neglect to nourish your body, you won't have the strength to manage your assets, feed your spirit, or control your thinking. If you don't control your thinking, you'll make poor decisions that impact your resources, and on it goes. It isn't enough to experience balance in any one, two, or even three areas of your life. You must gain control in all four to have a *total* quality life.

GET ON THE BIKE

My friend Steve enjoys bicycling as a fitness activity. Steve admits he's no Lance Armstrong, but he does ride nearly two thousand miles a year. I admire his willingness to stick with this activity month after month, including during inclement weather.

I once asked Steve what was the hardest part of his workout routine. He said, "That's simple. Getting on the bike. Every day I come up with a million reasons why I can't workout—it's too cold; I'm tired; I've got too much to do. I simply force myself to get on the bike. After that, it's easy."

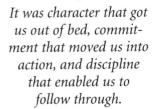

It was character that got us out of bed, commitment that moved us into action, and discipline that enabled us to follow through.

—Zig Ziglar

Right now you're probably thinking of a million reasons why you can't make the changes that will be required to experience a total quality life. TQL seems too far away. You're preoccupied with a big project at work. Things are busy at home. You're too tired right now. On and on your list will go. But there is a solution. You have to get on the bike and start riding. In other words, you must make the decision that you *will* improve the quality of your life, beginning now, and then take some action to get started.

Are you ready?

You won't be in it alone. I'll guide you in understanding and applying the principles of TQL throughout the remainder of this book. Each chapter will give you valuable information on how to make positive changes in your life. Along the way you'll be inspired by the examples of spiritual giants of ages past and modern-day heroes who have achieved total quality in their lives. Your satisfaction levels at home and work will rise dramatically; you'll be healthier in body, mind, and spirit; and you'll see your life change—for the better. You can do this!

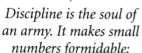

Discipline is the soul of an army. It makes small numbers formidable; procures success to the weak and esteem to all.

—George Washington

So let's begin by digging in deeper to the notion of quality to find out exactly what that might look like in *your* life.

STEPS TO TOTAL QUALITY

Take these five actions to solidify your resolve to pursue TQL.

1. List the areas of your life with which you are currently dissatisfied.
2. Begin keeping a TQL journal. For your first entry, write a one-paragraph description of your ideal life.
3. Determine to pursue TQL. Record your decision in writing, including today's date.
4. Identify three choices you can make that will begin the cycle of positive change in your life.
5. Tell at least one person that you have decided to make significant changes in your life to pursue total quality.

2

VISION

Your Benchmarks for
Total Quality

To achieve total quality, you must first
envision it. You alone will
determine the shape of your future.

"That car is a fine example of quality workmanship."

"That woman's quality; I knew it the first time I met her."

"It is the quality of time—not the quantity—that matters most."

When we talk about quality in any area of life, we may each have a different idea of what it means. Lifelong friends may have a heated argument over whether Ford or Chevy produces the best-quality truck. And don't even think about saying the word *Goldwing* to a Harley Davidson owner (or *Fat Boy* to a Honda rider). Each of us has some preconceived notion of what the term *quality* implies, but how many of us can articulate a clear definition of quality as applied to the place it matters most—our lives?

Before you can set out in search of TQL, you must have some idea of where you are going and what it will look like

> *Quality is never an accident; it is always the result of high intention, sincere effort, intelligent direction, and skillful execution; it represents the wise choice of many alternatives.*
>
> —William A. Foster

when you get there. You must have a vision of total quality. In this chapter, we'll examine several measures of quality that are used in various endeavors. We'll also look at the history of the concept of quality, and you'll have the opportunity to describe what quality will look like in your life—your vision of TQL.

DESCRIPTIONS OF QUALITY

Quality is defined in different ways in different disciplines. As we begin to apply the notion of quality to our lives, it will be helpful to take a quick look at some measures of quality that are used in various areas of human endeavor. By doing so we'll learn something about what quality is—and isn't—and we'll gather helpful ideas for forming a working definition of quality as it applies to our individual lives.

MEDICINE: QUALITY AS ABSENCE OF DISEASE

At first it may seem surprising to apply the term *quality* to something like health. Yet there are many objective measures of a person's physical or psychological well-being. In fact, the term *quality of life* (not the same as TQL) is derived from this field. When that term is applied in discussions concerning those suffering from debilitating or terminal illness, the conversation can become emotional. Yet we all can agree that our health may be better at some times and worse at others—giving it a greater or lesser degree of quality. I believe every person's life has inestimable value, regardless of the state of his or her health. However, I'm interested in finding a definition of quality as it applies to the area of medicine.

The Centers for Disease Control and Prevention (CDC) measure quality of life using a tool called Healthy Days Measures. The tool includes a series of questions that may not appear to be scientific but are useful in gauging the relative quality of a person's health. They are:

1. Would you say that in general your health is
    a. excellent
    b. very good
    c. good
    d. fair
    e. poor

2. Now thinking about your physical health, which includes physical illness and injury, for how many days during the past thirty days was your physical health not good?

3. Now thinking about your mental health, which includes stress, depression, and problems with emotions, for how many days during the past thirty days was your mental health not good?

4. During the past thirty days, for about how many days did poor physical or mental health keep you from doing your usual activities, such as self-care, work, or recreation?[1]

The CDC then asks ten more questions about recent pain, depression, anxiety, sleeplessness, vitality, and the cause, duration, and severity of a current activity limitation an individual may have.[2] Once the experts have gathered this information, they add the numbers of physically unhealthy and mentally unhealthy days and create a chart like this for the responder.

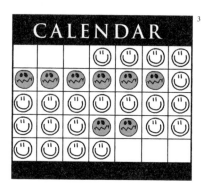

We might expect the CDC to come up with a more complex scientific formula for determining quality of life, but as you can see, the method is fairly simple. So one way of assessing quality of life is to evaluate it for pain, suffering, or limitations. A life free from pain or illness would have a higher degree of quality, by this definition. Again, I do not believe that a person who experiences illness or suffering has less value than a healthy person. Yet when assessing my life, I can see that the days on which I feel best physically and emotionally have a higher quality to me than do the days when I feel unwell.

Applying this definition as broadly as possible, consider the pain, problems, and stresses that affect your life. How might the quality of your life be improved if that pain were decreased or removed?

ECONOMICS: QUALITY AS STANDARD OF LIVING

Measuring quality using economic indicators would seem a simple matter. More money equals improved quality, right? It's not that simple. An economic system is more like an aquarium than a stockpile. Economists realize that subtle changes to one area of an economy—homebuilding, for example—will produce an effect on a seemingly unrelated area—such as interest rates. Quality is a complex issue and is surprisingly difficult to quantify in this discipline.

On a broad scale, economists seek to identify which groups of people enjoy the highest *standard of living*. This is a multifaceted concept that includes many factors other than income. Access to health care and education, length of the work week, environmental factors, and the stability of the economy are some factors considered when assessing the quality of a society from an economic point of view.

Complicating the matter further is that standards for quality in this area are subjective. For example, those who live in rural areas typically have a lower average income and less access to health care and education than do urbanites. Yet to many, the benefits of rural life—slower pace, less noise and pollution, more space—outweigh the perceived disadvantages.

The *Economist* magazine has an Intelligence Unit that claims to provide "a constant flow of analysis and forecasts on more than two hundred countries and eight key industries."[4] It has compiled a list of factors to help determine the standard of living in various countries around the world. They look at:

- material well-being
- health

- political stability and security
- family life
- community life
- job security
- political freedom
- gender equality

Interestingly, Ireland, Switzerland, and Norway topped the list for 2005. The United States and Canada came in thirteenth and fourteenth.[5]

Let's apply the economic definition of quality on an individual level.

What are the factors that might add up to total quality living for an individual? Would they be the same as those listed by the Economist? What elements might now be contributing to—or detracting from—your individual standard of living, your TQL?

MANUFACTURING: QUALITY AS PERFORMANCE

Manufacturers consider several factors when it comes to gauging the quality of their products, including: functionality, usability, reliability, and efficiency.[6] All that can be summarized by the single term *performance*. Manufacturers are concerned with delivering a product to the consumer that will consistently meet that customer's expectations. Whether the item is a new car, a golf club, or a vacuum cleaner, it must do what the manufacturer claims it will do—and do it well. Quality is consistent performance.

We apply the same measure as consumers. When I buy a new computer, I expect it to function, straight out of the box. If it doesn't, I expect the manufacturer to take it back or repair it. Even if my computer does what it's supposed to, is easy to use, and seldom needs repair, if it ran so slowly that I could do my work faster longhand, I'd consider the machine useless. The better an item performs its stated function, the higher the quality.

> *For we are God's workmanship, created in Christ Jesus to do good works, which God prepared in advance for us to do (Eph. 2:10).*

Let's consider this measure as it applies to life.

In what areas are you performing up to expectations—either your own or those of others? In which areas are you performing above expectations? In which areas of life is the quality low because your performance is lagging?

BUSINESS: QUALITY AS VALUE

In the business world, several variations on the concept of quality have emerged. Here are a few:

- "Attractive quality," what the customer would love but has not yet thought of (Noriaki Kano and others)
- "Products and services that meet or exceed customers' expectations" (Sam Walton)
- "Value to some person" (Gerald M. Weinberg)
- "A subjective term for which each person has his or her own definition" (American Society for Quality)[7]

The common denominator in each of these quality concepts is *value*. In the business world, to deliver quality is to deliver something useful or pleasing to the consumer in proportion to that consumer's expectation. By this definition, a wristwatch purchased either at Wal-Mart or at Cartier can be a quality item—one because it is inexpensive yet durable, the other because it is distinctive although highly expensive—because each *meets the expectation* of the consumer. It has value to someone.

By this measure, how would you rate the total quality of your life? Does it meet your own expectations? Do you feel you are getting enough in return for the time and energy you put into each area of your life? Are you a satisfied "customer"?

THE HISTORY OF TOTAL QUALITY

The quality movement traces its beginnings to the formation of guilds—trade associations formed to maintain standards of workmanship, protect mutual interests, and ensure ethical conduct. Though guilds weren't formalized until the Middle Ages, trade regulations can be traced back to the Code of Hammurabi, which prescribed the death penalty for builders whose buildings collapsed on people. Today associations such as the American Medical Society, the American Bar Association, and the National Association of Realtors could be considered guilds for these reasons: the state determines the qualifications for members, there is a strong affiliation among practitioners, and they self-regulate.[8] Formal guilds fell out of favor at the onset of the Industrial Revolution in the early nineteenth century. In their place, factories emphasized product inspection.

When the United States entered WWII, quality became essential for coordinating the war effort. Bullets manufactured in one state had to work in rifles manufactured in another state. To speed and simplify inspection processes, the military published specification standards and offered training in process-control techniques.

Following WWII, Japan sought to convert its factories from manufacturing war materials to manufacturing civilian goods for world trade. Initially unsuccessful due to shoddy workmanship, the Japanese solicited input from foreign companies and individuals, most notably W. Edwards Deming and Joseph M. Juran.

DEMING'S QUALITY REVOLUTION

Deming revolutionized Japanese production by teaching top managers how to improve design, product quality, testing, and sales. His message was that improving quality would reduce expenses and increase both productivity and market share.[9] Several Japanese manufacturers applied Deming's techniques and experienced phenomenal growth, far surpassing

PIERCING VISION: BILLY GRAHAM

Billy Graham is arguably the most influential person of the twentieth century. He has preached the gospel to more people in live audiences than anyone else in history—more than 210 million people in at least 185 countries and territories. Hundreds of millions more have been reached through television, video, film, and web casts.

This son of a North Carolina dairy farmer has appeared on the Gallup Poll's "Ten Most Admired Men in the World" a record 43 times.

What accounts for this success? Graham's life of total quality is guided by a clear vision. He wrote, "My one purpose in life is to help people find a personal relationship with God, which, I believe, comes through knowing Christ."

U.S. competitors. He is regarded as having had a greater impact on Japanese business than any other individual not of Japanese heritage.[10]

Despite his success overseas, Deming remained mostly unknown in America until 1980, when he was featured in an NBC program documenting Japan's great strides in outperforming U.S. manufacturers. As a result of that appearance, Ford Motor Company retained Deming's services. By 1986 Ford had become the most profitable American car company thanks in large part to Deming's philosophies of management and quality. Do you remember the slogan "Quality Is Job 1"?

> *Quality means doing it right when no one is looking.*
>
> —Henry Ford

DEMING'S DIRECTIVES AND DISEASES

Deming offered fourteen points for transforming management and increasing effectiveness:

1. Create constancy of purpose for the improvement of product and service, with the aim to become competitive, stay in business, and provide jobs.
2. Adopt a new philosophy of cooperation in which everybody wins, and put it into practice by teaching it to employees, customers, and suppliers.
3. Cease dependence on mass inspection to achieve quality. Instead, improve the process and build quality into the product in the first place.
4. End the practice of awarding business on the basis of price tag alone. Instead, minimize total

cost in the long run. Move toward a single supplier for any one item, based on a long-term relationship of loyalty and trust.

5. Constantly improve the system of production, service, and planning of any activity.

6. Institute training for skills.

7. Adopt and institute leadership for the management of people, recognizing their different abilities, capabilities, and aspiration. The aim of leadership should be to help people, machines, and gadgets do a better job.

8. Drive out fear and build trust so everyone can work more effectively.

9. Break down barriers between departments. Abolish competition, and build a win-win system of cooperation within the organization.

10. Eliminate slogans, exhortations, and targets asking for zero defects or new levels of productivity. Such exhortations only create adversarial relationships, as the bulk of the causes of low quality and low productivity belong to the system and thus lie beyond the power of the workforce.

11. Eliminate numerical goals, numerical quotas, and management by objectives.

12. Remove barriers that rob people of joy in their work. This will mean abolishing the annual rating or merit system that ranks people and creates competition and conflict.

13. Institute a vigorous program of education and self-improvement.

14. Put everybody in the company to work to accomplish the transformation. The transformation is everybody's job.

Deming also had a list of Seven Deadly Diseases that he believed organizations must avoid:

1. Lack of constancy of purpose
2. Emphasis on short-term profits
3. Evaluation by performance, merit rating, or annual review of performance
4. Mobility of management
5. Running a company on visible figures alone
6. Excessive medical costs
7. Excessive costs of a warranty, fueled by lawyers who work for contingency fees.

Under a lesser category of obstacles, Deming placed the following:

1. Neglecting long-range planning
2. Relying on technology to solve problems
3. Seeking examples to follow rather than developing solutions
4. Offering excuses such as "Our problems are different"[11]
5. Other companies and CEOs stepped up and integrated Deming's principles, ultimately developing what came to be known as Total Quality Management or TQM.

TQM

International Organization for Standardization (ISO)[12] defines Total Quality Management as: "a management approach for an organization, centered on quality, based on the participation of all its members and aiming at longterm success through customer satis-faction, and benefits to all members of the organization and to society."[13]

TQM focuses on getting all employees to aim toward a continual increase in customer

> *Associate yourself with people of good quality, for it is better to be alone than in bad company.*
>
> —George Washington

satisfaction and lower production costs. By now the term TQM has lost a certain level of popularity. Its practices, however, continue.

How does the history of total quality management relate to your life? Have you made yourself accountable to a code or certain objective standards? Do you consider self-improvement to be "Job 1"? Which of Deming's directives do you most need to apply to your self-management? Which of Deming's diseases might be hampering you from realizing your life goals?

THE COST OF TOTAL QUALITY

Another phrase frequently used in discussions about quality, often incorrectly, is *cost of quality*. The cost of quality is not how much one must invest to create a quality product. Rather, it is the cost of *not* creating quality. When a chair lacks quality, for example, eventually consumers will complain or refuse to buy that model. At that point the company must do some combination of the following:

- recall and destroy all defective chairs
- modify or rework the faulty chairs (including sending out replacement parts)
- reinspect the low-quality chairs and the replacements
- retest low-quality chairs and replacements
- review raw materials and components of the faulty chairs
- downgrade consumer expectations[14]

By itself, any one of these options is expensive. Combine two or three, and the chair manufacturer must question whether it can afford to continue to make chairs at all, let alone those that don't meet consumer standards.

Men acquire a particular quality by constantly acting a particular way. We become just by performing just actions, temperate by performing temperate actions, brave by performing brave actions.

—Aristotle

The preceding discussion on the cost of quality presupposes a lack of quality in a product but a high level of quality or integrity, in the company or person responsible. What happens when the roles are reversed?

Quality products have often been produced by those who lack a quality of life. For example, Henry Ford (1863–1947) revolutionized American transportation with the introduction of his Model T. He was also an outspoken anti-Semite. Wallace Carothers (1896–1937), an American chemist credited with inventing nylon, committed suicide at age forty.[15] Samuel Morse (1791–1872), inventor of the Morse code, was an avid supporter of slavery and opposed immigration of Irish Catholics, believing their coming would eventually enable the Pope to rule America.[16] Countless others—teachers, religious leaders, lawmakers—have tarnished or destroyed their positive legacies by demonstrating a lack of quality (integrity, sound judgment, and so forth) in their personal lives. While they have done good things, their lives have not matched their products.

What is the cost of quality as applied to your life? Take a moment to reflect upon your personal life, family, work, finances, and relationships. In which life areas, if any, are you failing to meet your own expectations or to deliver value to others? What will be the cost to you—and to others—if you do not address the need for quality improvement? What is the cost of TQL?

EXAMPLES OF TOTAL QUALITY

A quality life has the potential to impact others far more than do quality products. Let's take a quick look at a few stunning examples of quality lives.

MOTHER TERESA

Mother Teresa (1910–1997) felt the call of God on her life at age twelve and became a nun and then a teacher in a convent in Calcutta from 1931 to 1948. She simply couldn't ignore the poverty outside the convent walls. So she successfully appealed to the Vatican to start her own order, the Missionaries of Charity, to care for (in her words) "the hungry, the naked, the homeless, the crippled, the blind, the lepers, all those people who feel unwanted, unloved, uncared for throughout society, people that have become a burden to the society and are shunned by everyone."[17]

As a result of her example of selfless service, the Missionaries of Charity operate orphanages, AIDS hospice centers, leper homes, and charity homes. They also provide care for refugees, natural disaster victims, the blind, aged, poor, and homeless on six continents. Though she received many prestigious awards for her work, including the Nobel Peace Prize, Mother Teresa remained focused on her calling and those she served. She said,

> At the end of our lives, we will not be judged by how many diplomas we have received, how much money we have made or how many great things we have done. We will be judged by "I was hungry and you gave me to eat. I was naked and you clothed me. I was homeless and you took me in." Hungry not only for bread—but hungry for love. Naked not only for clothing—but naked of human dignity and respect. Homeless not only for want of a room of bricks—but homeless because of rejection. This is Christ in distressing disguise.[18]
>
> When a poor person dies of hunger, it has not happened because God did not take care of him or her. It has happened because neither you nor I wanted to give that person what he or she needed.[19]

To Mother Teresa, a quality life was everything, but some people aren't even aware they're demonstrating a quality life.

HATTIE MAY WIATT

The congregation hall of Grace Baptist Church in Philadelphia was packed with people attending church services. The space was so small for the growing number of churchgoers that the deacons had to issue admission tickets weeks in advance.

Sunday school was no different. The schoolrooms were over-crowded with children, and some had to wait outside for their turn to get in. Eight-year-old Hattie May Wiatt waited at the gate one Sunday in 1884. She held her

The quality of expectations determines the quality of our action.

—Andre Godin

books and her offering money, but somehow seeing the place so full made her hesitant. Dr. Russell H. Conwell, pastor of Grace Baptist Church, passed by to attend the Sunday school and saw little Hattie. He led her inside and found a chair for her in that crowded classroom. It marked the beginning of his friendship with this girl and her family.

The following day, Dr. Conwell saw Hattie on her way to school. Just to get a conversation going, Dr. Conwell told Hattie about the new plan to build a larger Sunday school room, to which she replied, "I hope you will. It is so crowded that I am afraid to go there alone." Days later, news came to Dr. Conwell that Hattie was very sick. He paid her a visit and prayed for her. Two years later, ten-year-old Hattie died of diphtheria.

After the funeral, Hattie's mother handed Dr. Conwell a purse that contained her daughter's savings amounting to fifty-seven cents and a note in child's handwriting that read, "This is to help build the little church bigger so more children can go to

Sunday school." Dr. Conwell presented the gift to the church deacons, who exchanged the coins for fifty-seven pennies.

As the number of church members grew and the news of Hattie's fifty-seven cents hit the headlines, Grace Baptist Church used Hattie's inspiration to purchase a property offered at a discounted price and a down payment amounting to only fifty-four cents. Five years later, the church conducted its first worship service on the new property in a new building—with more than nine thousand worshipers in attendance.

Just over twenty years after Hattie's death, the church was able to pay off the debt. Fifty-four of the original fifty-seven cents were returned to the Baptist Temple Church as a gift. Dr. Conwell decided to keep and exhibit all fifty-four cents to serve as a stirring reminder of how a child's love inspired a congregation to unite and give selflessly.

Today, the Baptist Temple Church, Temple University, and Temple Hospital still stand as witnesses to Hattie May Wiatt's expression of a quality life.[20]

YOUR TQL

Billy Graham, Mother Teresa, Hattie May Wiatt, and you have one thing in common: the desire for a quality life. The rest of this book is dedicated to helping you achieve that goal.

But remember that TQL is an individualized pursuit. Your total quality life will likely look different from mine, just as quality is measured differently for doctors, auto manufacturers, and retailers. So before you begin the quest for TQL, you must assess both where you are and where you hope to go.

Define for yourself the kind of life you wish to live. Then you will be ready to pursue TQL in each of the four critical areas of life.

Which model of quality best fits your life? What will be the benchmark for your TQL? What directives or diseases are most pressing? What is the cost of your TQL—or the cost of failing to achieve it?

STEPS TO TOTAL QUALITY

Take these five actions to solidify your resolve to pursue TQL.

1. Review the descriptions of quality listed in this chapter and choose those that you find most helpful in defining your TQL.
2. Review the list of Deming's Directives and identify those that you most need to adopt.
3. Review Deming's Diseases and Obstacles and identify any that currently hinder you from living a quality life.
4. Consider the cost of quality in your life. Identify the sacrifices you will have to make in order to achieve TQL.
5. Consider the examples of TQL listed in this chapter and others that you can name. Identify a role model for yourself and read more about that person's life.

CRITICAL
LIFE SPHERES

Quality is pervasive; it must permeate
every area of your life.

You must achieve TQL in your—
Mind
Body
Resources
Spirit

3

MIND

❦

TOTAL QUALITY
THOUGHT

Thoughts become attitudes. Attitudes become actions.
Actions become habits. Therefore, the key
to controlling your life is to control your mind.

The word *repent* brings to mind all sorts of images—from
a street prophet wearing a sandwich sign to a wild-eyed
Puritan preaching hellfire and brimstone. We chuckle at the
one and cringe at the other, taking neither too seriously. But
repentance isn't just about religion, and it has little to do with
long-haired pseudo-prophets. Repentance is about the mind
and heart. According to John Piper, to repent "is to experience
a change of the mind's perceptions and dispositions and
purposes."[1]

Whatever you may think about pop psychologist Dr. Phil,
one of his catch phrases helps illustrate the idea of repentance.
When his guests have finished telling their tragic stories of
how they've dealt with their children's lack of respect or their
boss's lack of appreciation, Dr. Phil often responds, in his
Texas drawl, with, "How's that workin' for you?" Usually the

answer is, "Not very well." When a behavior or attitude isn't "working" for us, we need to repent—to change our thinking.

That makes repentance a big part of the Total Quality Life. If you are to experience TQL, it's likely that you will need to make certain changes in outlook and in thought patterns. You'll need a change of mind. To maintain TQL, you'll need to develop and consistently practice the thought patterns that produce total quality.

MENTAL DETOX

In 2004 film director Morgan Spurlock became a human guinea pig. For thirty days he ate food only from McDonald's restaurants, and he documented his experiment on video. Here are the highlights:

- His average intake was 5,000 calories per day.
- He gained 24.5 pounds (from 185.5 to 210).
- He gained 7 percent body fat (from 11 to 18 percent).
- His cholesterol went up 65 points.
- It took him two months to get his cholesterol and liver functions back to normal and more than a year to lose the weight.[2]

Spurlock's experiment proved that the quality of one's diet has a direct impact upon the quality of one's health.

What is true for the body is true for the mind, as well. Just as Spurlock assaulted his body with fast food, we regularly assault our minds with a jumble of useless, even harmful, information that clouds and distorts our thinking. We barely have time to take in, let alone make sense of, the thousands of bits of information we receive each day. The quality of our intellectual intake has a direct impact on the quality of our mental and emotional health.

God designed our minds to work best when we follow the instructions given in our owner's manual—the Bible. Unfortunately,

Repentance is another name for aspiration.

—Henry Ward Beecher

in today's world there is so much clutter going through our minds that our thinking is cloudy and distorted. For us to think in a way that leads to healthy living, we need to have healthy thoughts. We need to learn to think the right thoughts just as we must learn to eat the right foods. Just as a body may need to be cleansed of toxins that harm it and impede its ability to function, your mind may need to be cleansed of thoughts and information that hinder you from living optimally. Your TQL begins with a mind diet.

Many diets begin by detoxifying the body for three days. This usually is the most difficult part of the diet, but it is essential for success. To detoxify your mind, you will need a period of reduced stimulation. That means no TV, no radio, and no Internet. To cleanse your mind of the many powerful thoughts and images that have been planted there, you'll need to maintain this semi-seclusion for seven full days. Don't worry, the world will go on whether you know what's happening in the news or not.

Don't cheat on your diet. Do not reread old trade magazines or watch videos or DVDs. Cleanse your mind through healthy activities like being alone, spending time outdoors, chatting with friends, or praying. You may listen to music that is simple and preferably instrumental, and you may read inspirational and uplifting books or the Bible. (See the Resource Guide at the end of this book for suggestions.) Now is the time to clear your mind, ridding it of the toxic information that bombards it every day, and filling it with what is good, positive, and peaceful.

AN INVENTORY OF YOUR MIND

Remember the definition of repentance? It is a change of mind. Once you've completed your mental detox, you'll have the clarity to see exactly what needs to be changed. Take a look at where you are right now and where you want to go.

According to the Bible, each individual has been created in the image of Almighty God. This doesn't mean that we look like him, but that we have a unique personality, an eternal soul, and the ability to think abstractly, to be creative, and to make moral judgments. In short, God has made each one of us with unique gifts, talents, and abilities that we can choose to use for the benefit of ourselves and others.

A QUICK TURN: ZACCHAEUS

In New Testament times, the terms *tax collector* and *sinner* were always used in the same breath. The Rome-appointed tax collectors were notorious for overcharging and pocketing the surplus. So, when Jesus invited himself to Zacchaeus' home for dinner, Jesus was associating with the worst of sinners.

But Zacchaeus dramatically repented. He said, "Here and now I give half of my possessions to the poor, and if I have cheated anybody out of anything, I will pay back four times the amount."

That was repentance—a change of heart that became a gateway to a Total Quality Life.

Take a few moments to consider your life. Think about what's not working for you—what you've been doing that you don't want to do anymore, and what you haven't been doing that you want to start—in the following areas.

Spiritual. Have you thought that spirituality is only for the weak? Do you spend time in prayer, meditation, and thanksgiving? Do you read the Bible and other inspirational material?

Mental. Do you believe that since your school days are behind you, you no longer need to read or learn? Does the material you

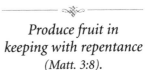

Produce fruit in keeping with repentance (Matt. 3:8).

choose to read stretch your thinking? Do you explore new subjects just to broaden your understanding?

Physical. Is your weight under control? If so, do you also exercise regularly? Have you tried a new sport lately? How about a new machine at the gym? Have you taken a walk on a new trail or gone outside early in the morning just to see the sunrise?

Family. Do you feel like your family life is pretty good? Have you called your mother, father, siblings in the last month? Do your kids see you only at bedtime because you work late so often? Does your spouse feel appreciated?

Professional. Do you feel as though everything's running smoothly at the office and you've arrived? When was the last time you learned something new about your career? Are you doing your job a certain way because that's the way it's always been done?

Community. Do you have a "they don't bother us; we don't bother them" attitude toward those around you? Do you know your neighbors? Have you volunteered for anything in the past year?

These questions are not intended to make you feel guilty or discouraged. They're prompts to get you thinking about what you're doing and how you want your life to look in the future.

MAKING HEALTHY CHOICES

One of the things I've learned over the years as I've tried to live a healthy lifestyle is that every choice matters. I can tell myself, "Oh, this piece of cheesecake won't affect my waist-line," but it will. I'm not saying you should never have dessert or junk food, but that you should realize the price you may pay by choosing it. If you make unhealthy choices more often, the price goes up, as Morgan Spurlock demonstrated in his documentary.

The same is true with your thoughts and attitudes. Just like you're in charge of what you put into your mouth, you're also in charge of what you put into your mind. Have you ever heard a child say, "You're not the boss of me!" Well, you *are* the boss of your mind—you have control over what goes into it. Just as a bite of cheesecake isn't going to turn your body to flab, watching one sitcom on TV or reading a suspense novel now and then isn't going to turn your mind to mush. But watching sitcoms every night or reading only pulp fiction will eventually take its

Nobody can go back and start a new beginning, but anyone can start today and make a new ending.

—Maria Robinson

From Slave Trader to Saint: John Newton

John Newton's godly mother died when he was seven. At age eleven he left school and joined his father's shipping company. He described his young self as an "infidel," "libertine," and "wretch." He was forced to enlist on a British man-of-war seven years later, but eventually deserted. Recaptured after his desertion, the disgraced sailor was exchanged to the crew of a slave ship bound for Africa.

While he was on a voyage, a terrifying storm came up, and Newton was afraid he was going to die. He determined that he would place his trust in God. Although he survived the storm, Newton continued as captain of a slave ship. The deplorable conditions of slavery eventually caused him to give up slave trading to become a minister and advocate for abolition for the last forty-three years of his life.

At eighty-two Newton said, "My memory is nearly gone, but I remember only two things, that I am a great sinner and that Christ is a great Savior." That sentiment is poetically summed up in his famous hymn, "Amazing Grace."

Newton's dramatic change of heart was the foundation not only for his own life change but became an example of right thinking that has inspired millions of people.

toll on your thinking. So how can you integrate media into your life in a way that benefits your mind rather than harms it? You must take control of your choices.

No doubt you've been to a shopping mall with a food court that offers a wide variety of choices—from Chinese to Greek to Mexican, with all the fast-food standards thrown in. Typically, you have to look closely to find a healthy choice among all the fat and sugar offered. But if you're persistent, you usually can find something.

The same is true for your intellectual life. Now that you've decided to stop the patterns of thought that aren't working, you need to replace those attitudes with their opposites. After all, repentance doesn't mean stopping one thing only to do something almost like it. Repentance is about making a complete change—doing a one-eighty.

Think back over the list of thoughts, attitudes, or assumptions that are not working. Take the professional arena, for example. It may be that you are good at your job, and you know it. Probably your boss knows it, too. Are you feeling a little smug? Take a closer look at that attitude. What would happen if you replaced the this-company-owes-me attitude with an eagerness to learn and to improve things where you work? What if you took a new person under your wing not just to teach him or her but to hear new ideas and consider new options. That's choosing a healthy alternative to mental junk food. It's on-the-job repentance.

> *We will have to repent in this generation not merely for the vitriolic words and actions of the bad people, but for the appalling silence of the good people.*
>
> —Martin Luther King, Jr.

Here are some tips for building healthy thought choices into other areas of your mind's diet.

TELEVISION

When you turn on the tube, be sure to evaluate the content you choose to view. Does the program actively engage you intellectually? Do you respect this program and its creators?[3] Is the message of this show valuable in some way? Is the message of this show clear? Does this show challenge you somehow?[4]

BOOKS

Amazon.com is a great place to read reviews of any book before you buy it. Just make sure you read more than the first two or three, since some authors get their friends and families to write glowing reviews whether the book deserves it or not. To stretch your mind and broaden your literary horizons, check out www.anova.org for a list of great books by nearly 250 authors. Many texts are available online.

Business Book Review offers summaries of the best business books for a small fee. Visit their Website to learn more: www.businessbookreview.com. *Business Week* Online posts numerous reviews of business books. You can find them at www.businessweek.com/lifestyle/books.htm.

PEOPLE

Just as you need to make wise choices with media, you'll also need to be selective about your friends and others with whom you associate. Choose people who motivate you, who encourage you and build you up. If you want to create a TQL, you don't have time to waste with negative, uninspiring people.

ONE DAY AT A TIME

TQL is a daily journey, and even the most motivated people stumble sometimes. When that happens, don't worry, and don't beat yourself up. You're making significant changes to your life; you're to be commended for your efforts and your perseverance. But remember, every choice matters. Every minute presents an opportunity to make a different choice. No matter what your mother told you, you don't have to clean your plate—at least not when it comes to your intellectual intake. Just because you've started a book or a television program doesn't mean you have to give it the next hour of your life. You can always choose to stop and turn around. You control what goes into your mind. What will you choose today?

STEPS TO TOTAL QUALITY
Take these five actions to solidify your resolve to pursue TQL.

1. Undergo a one-week period of mental detoxification as outlined in this chapter.
2. Take an inventory of your mind as described in this chapter. Spend one hour reflecting on your findings.
3. Record your mental intake for one week, listing all media content that you consume. Analyze whether each choice has added value or detracted from your quest for TQL.
4. Create a media map for your future, listing the media that you will consume—and that which you will avoid.
5. List three negative attitudes that you wish to eliminate from your thinking and three positive attitudes that you wish to adopt. Reflect on this list weekly for six weeks, analyzing your progress.

4

BODY

TOTAL QUALITY HEALTH

Diet, rest, and exercise form the iron triangle
of good health. Neglect any one of these,
and you can never enjoy the Total Quality Life.

My friend Mary thrives on being told she can't do something—not something bad or illegal, but anything that seems beyond her ability. She loves a challenge. A few years ago, Mary decided that even though she'd never really been a runner, she was going to participate in the Chicago marathon. She bought running shoes designed for someone with her build and running style, changed her diet to enhance her stamina, and followed a training schedule religiously for nine months. She read books to learn how to think while she was running. The week of the race she packed and repacked her gear, checked the weather forecasts and made sure she had everything she needed for every possible contingency.

The day of the race dawned crisp and clear—and Mary was prepared. At the starting line, she headed for the back of the pack, knowing competitive runners (as opposed to participants) hate it when amateurs get in their way. The crack of the starter's pistol startled her into motion, and twenty minutes later, Mary crossed the starting line behind twenty-thousand other marathoners and began the race.

Making her way through the streets of Chicago, Mary was amazed at the friendliness of other runners and at the wild cheering and enthusiastic encouragement of the crowd. At about mile eighteen, she fell into step with a girl named Lisa, who seemed to be going at about Mary's pace. The two of them became friends—in the same way that two soldiers sharing a foxhole become friends—and distracted themselves from the pain that had crept up on them by practicing their "queenly" waves as they plodded down Michigan Avenue. Finally the balloon arch that marked the finish line came into view. Mary and Lisa grabbed hold of each other's hands and pulled each other forward, both giving all they had to cross the line. Since it's against the rules to finish hand-in-hand, at the last moment they dropped hands and crossed the line only a split second apart.

Life expectancy would grow by leaps and bounds if green vegetables smelled as good as bacon.

—Doug Larson

Mary told me the experience of completing 26.2 miles and having a finisher's medal placed around her neck was like nothing she'd ever known before. Later she heard that a new world record had been set in that race. She said, "Where else could I have been in the same event as a world-class runner?" It was the accomplishment of a lifetime for her.

What do you suppose would have happened to Mary if she had simply awakened one morning and decided to run a marathon that day? What if she'd gobbled down a plate of bacon and eggs, laced up the old sneakers she wore to mow the lawn, thrown on an old T-shirt, and headed for the starting line? Her lack of training, proper equipment, and appropriate diet would have sealed her fate, and the day would have ended in disappointment and failure.

In a way Mary was looking for a total quality marathon experience. She had a goal in mind, and she did all she could to assure that outcome. Like Mary, you'll need a healthy, well-disciplined body to reach your goal of Total Quality Life. The remainder of this chapter will provide you with tools you'll need to do that. Now, as the commercial says, I'm not a doctor and I don't even play one on TV, so I won't presume to tell you the best way for you to get into shape. Only your personal physician knows you well enough to make that recommendation. I do, however, have some health tips that apply to all of us.

THE ONLY DIET THAT WORKS

Every publisher knows the best time to release a diet book is in January. That's when consumers look to make lifestyle changes and drop a few pounds; and they invariably reach for the latest, easiest, and least painful way to do it. Estimates on what Americans spend on diet books each year range from thirty to forty-two billion dollars.[1]

According to Pamela Cekola, R.D., and Ruchi Mathur, M.D., here are some things to beware of as you look for a program to help you achieve a total quality body. Steer clear of any regimen that promises or requires these:

- fast weight loss
- a quick fix
- claims that sound too good to be true
- foods identified as "good" or "bad"
- fewer than 1,000 calories daily
- a required vitamin or mineral supplement or food product
- elimination of a major food group (such as carbohydrates, fats, or proteins)
- a lack of long-term randomized scientific studies that prove the diet is safe and effective.[2]

So with hundreds of diet books on the market and a weight-loss center in nearly every strip mall, why aren't we all living at our ideal weight? The reason is simple. We don't want to follow the one weight-loss plan that is *guaranteed* to work: Eat less and exercise more. The U.S. Food and Drug Administration made this statement: "To lose weight safely and keep it off requires long-term changes in daily eating and exercise habits. Many experts recommend a goal of losing about a pound a week. A modest reduction of 500 calories per day will achieve this goal, since a total reduction of 3,500 calories is required to lose a pound of fat. An important way to lower your calorie intake is to learn and practice healthy eating habits."[3]

It sounds easy, doesn't it? Yet most of us find it impossible to make the lifestyle adjustments that result in good health. You can change that, at least for yourself. Let me give you five simple steps you can take to implement this simple-but-not-so-easy plan for maintaining total quality fitness.

EVALUATE FOODS BASED ON COLOR

Have you ever noticed that most junk foods bear little resemblance to their natural counterparts? For example, have you ever seen a block of cheddar cheese the color of one of those processed cheese curls or cheese puffs? While we're at it, exactly what is "nacho" cheese? And have you ever observed a blue raspberry growing in a raspberry patch? Dietary experts tell us that natural, unprocessed food is best for us.

Here's a simple way to evaluate the nutritional impact of the foods you choose: the brighter the color, the more nutrient-packed the food is. This assumes, of course, that the color appears in nature, and that the color is natural and not added or enhanced. I could quote any number of scientific studies to support this statement, but you already know it's true. Natural

CHOICES FOR LIFE: DANIEL

Daniel was probably a teenager when he was taken into slavery in ancient Babylon. To make matters worse, the godly Jew was thrown into a frat house at the state-sponsored university for future leaders. But this young man and his three friends were not about to let pagan Babylon corrupt their faith—or their diet.

When offered the king's royal food and wine, Daniel offered a test to prove his own diet was healthier. Eating only vegetables and water for ten days, Daniel and his companions were visibly healthier than those who ate the rich but unhealthy diet of the king's table.

Daniel's faith and healthy diet led to him being promoted within the Babylonian government; later he became one of three presidents.

foods look the best and are the best for you. Dorothy Gault-McNemee, M.D., said it well in her book *God's Diet*: "If God didn't make it, don't eat it!"[4]

So the next time you're tempted by a highly processed food, choose a natural one instead. Instead of a candy bar, have some peanut butter or raisins. Instead of something blue, try a sweet and juicy orange.

GET MORE REST

Do you consider yourself a workaholic, or perhaps highly committed to your job? Answer yes or no to the following questions to validate your answer.

- Do I regularly work six or seven days a week?
- Do I regularly work ten or more hours a day?
- Do I often work through lunch?
- Do I think about my job even while I'm on vacation?
- Do I answer work-related e-mail or voice mail at home in the evenings or on weekends?
- Do I typically talk mostly about work with my spouse, family, and friends?[5]
- Do I have a hobby?
- Do I have friends outside the office?
- Do I laugh and smile as much as I used to?[6]

Your answers are telling, aren't they? If your family only sees you between ten at night and six in the morning or if you can't remember if you have a hobby, you're in serious need of rest. Rest is not for the lazy—it is for those who want to maximize their productivity. It is vital for your body to function as it should.

In *A Passionate Life*, Mike Breen and Walt Kallestad write about God's plan for work and rest, which he modeled in creation. God created man and woman on the sixth day. He set them in a garden full of wild and wonderful creatures and delicious foods to eat. He gave them instruction on caring for the animals and plants in the garden. He told them to be fruitful. And he wasn't talking just about having children.

But on the first full day of existence for Adam and Eve, God rested. So did Adam and Eve. All creation took a well-deserved break in activity. This was our first full day as humans—a day of rest. After the hard work of being created, the next thing we did was hang out with God for a whole day. Then our responsibilities began. We need only go to the first page of our story to see that. From this we see an important life principle: We are to work from our rest, not rest from our work.[7]

Do you not know that your body is a temple of the Holy Spirit, who is in you, whom you have received from God? . . . Therefore honor God with your body (1 Cor. 6:19–20).

When was the last time you scheduled a day—or even a few hours—for rest? And by rest I don't necessarily mean a nap, though that may be what you need. Ask yourself what activities refresh and reenergize you. Know what charges your battery and then do it.

THE BIGGEST 'LOSER': ERIK CHOPIN

Thirty-five-year-old Erik Chopin weighed 407 pounds when he arrived on the set of the reality TV program "The Biggest Loser," the show that follows contestants as they adopt a healthy diet and rigorous exercise regimen for the chance to win $25,000 as "The Biggest Loser."

The Long Island deli owner—not the best profession for weight loss—lost 124 pounds at "The Biggest Loser" ranch and an additional ninety pounds after returning home. Winning the contest, he weighed in at 193 pounds giving him a total weight loss of 214 pounds or meaning he lost over 52 percent of his former weight.

By stressing the value of healthy eating and exercise rather than fad diets, surgery, or diet pills, this "loser" demonstrated that total quality health is an achievable goal.

EXERCISE CONSISTENTLY

Most of us admit we need more exercise than we get. In case you're unsure of the value of exercise, consider these facts:

- Exercise is good for your brain. In one study, adults who walked three times a week for up to forty-five minutes saw an 11 percent improvement on tests measuring decision-making ability.[8]

- Aerobic exercise and strength training may be as effective for treating depression as drugs and therapy. In one study, depressed exercisers experienced significantly lower relapse rates than participants who had taken medication.[9]

- Physically active men and women may be 40 to 50 percent less likely to develop colon cancer than sedentary people.
- Active women may be 30 to 40 percent less likely to develop breast cancer.[10]
- Multiple short sessions of exercise are just as effective for fitness and weight loss as one long session.[11]
- Lifting weights improves balance. In a one-year study, middle-aged women who didn't exercise showed an 8.5 percent decline in balance. Those who lifted weights improved their balance by 14 percent.[12]

You know exercise is good for you, but it's not easy to fit into your schedule. I remember hearing a popular motivational speaker say that if he could get himself out of bed within ten minutes of the alarm going off he knew he could get himself onto his treadmill. I know from experience that getting up and moving improves the quality of my day. Knowing I've given my body what it needs to function at optimal levels makes me more alert, gives me more energy, and helps me deal with the day's inevitable stress.

RECOGNIZE AND REDUCE STRESS

Stress is a fact of life for nearly everyone. We know we are under too much stress but often feel helpless to do anything about it. Some researchers estimate that stress-related issues account for 40 to 80 percent of all doctor visits. Stress may be the culprit in many cases of heart disease, anxiety attacks, mood swings, colds, flu, depression, high blood pressure, eating disorders, chronic pain, and other common ailments and illnesses.[13]

Without question, stress reduction is in order. But how can you accomplish it? Here are several ideas:

- Moderate exercise is the best way to alleviate stress. A walk at lunchtime will help you to concentrate through the afternoon.
- Drink lots of water.
- Break tasks into manageable units.
- Reduce noise levels. Close your office door, turn off the TV or MP3 player for a while and bask in silence.
- Don't waste time gossiping.
- Forgive quickly; judge less.
- Simplify your surroundings; get rid of clutter.
- Count your blessings.
- Offer compliments to your server in a restaurant or an often-overlooked assistant.
- Consider your calendar full. Say no.
- Be as kind to yourself as you would be to your best friend.
- Consider any failure as an opportunity to learn something new.[14]

These ideas may sound simplistic, but I assure you they work. Stress is often caused by the aggregate effect of several small factors. Eliminating or reducing them one by one is an effective way to reduce your overall stress level.

QUIT SMOKING

There is no need to pile on more data about the ill effects of smoking on health. We all know smoking kills. There is no place for it in a TQL. If you don't smoke, don't start. If you do smoke, stop.

I have to exercise in the morning before my brain figures out what I'm doing.

—Marsha Doble

Because nicotine is an addictive substance, many people find this lifestyle change the hardest one to make. If you have had difficulty in quitting smoking, talk with your doctor now about developing a smoking cessation plan.

THE DOCTOR IS IN

Reestablishing and maintaining physical health is a vital part of a TQL. For many people, establishing the habits that sustain good health is mostly a matter of resolve. We know we need to eat less, exercise more, and get proper rest; we simply must make the daily changes that allow us to act on those good intentions. For some of us, however, there are more significant health problems involved, problems that require the advice or treatment of a physician. If you have not had a physical checkup recently, now is the time to get one. Consult your dentist also. This is important even if you do not have a known health problem. Don't wait for a toothache or a broken bone. Early detection of problems is the best way to live a healthy, total quality life.

Is it possible to make the changes that lead to good health? You bet it is. A Total Quality Life requires maintaining total quality fitness, and that's something you can do.

STEPS TO TOTAL QUALITY
Take these five actions to solidify your resolve to pursue TQL.

1. Schedule an appointment for a complete physical examination with your doctor. Ask, "What do I need to do to improve my health?"
2. Choose one positive change you will make concerning your diet. List the choice along with today's date in your TQL journal.
3. Choose a form of exercise that appeals to you such as walking, tennis, or biking. Set a goal for the number and duration of workouts that you will do in the next month.
4. Log the number of hours that you sleep each night for two weeks. If the average is less than seven hours, identify one change you can make to increase the amount of time that you sleep.
5. Identify three stress-busting activities that work for you. Make a specific plan to engage in one or more of those activities at least twice a week.

5

RESOURCES

❦

TOTAL QUALITY
FINANCES

You can have it all—
if you are willing to give it all away.

B y the time they're sixty-five years old, half of all Americans
will be flat broke." I recently heard this startling statement
on the radio. While I was skeptical at first, after digging a bit
deeper into financial statistics, I no longer doubt it. Here's why:

- The average American household with at least one
  credit card has about $9,200 in credit card debt.
- Forty-two percent of Americans pay just the minimum
  or no payments on their credit card debt.[1]
- In 2005 more than 2 million individuals filed for
  bankruptcy, up 1.1 million from ten years ago.[2]
- About 43 percent of American families spend more
  than they earn, $1.22 spent for every dollar earned.[3]
- More than 1.8 million homeowners have outstanding
  loans that equal 100 percent or more of the value of
  their homes.[4]

- The credit card industry mailed more than six billion credit card offers in 2005, an average of six offers per household per month.[5]
- Credit card late fee penalties totaled more than $11 billion in 2005.[6]
- The average amount financed for new car purchases was just over $26,000 in 2005.[7]
- In 2005 the rate of personal savings in the United States dipped below 0 percent for the first time since the Great Depression, hitting -0.5 percent.[8]
- As of 2004, a typical credit card purchase cost 12 to18 percent more than cash.[9]

The statistic that clinched it for me, though, was this one: in 2004, the average personal wealth of a fifty-year-old American was less than $40,000, including home equity. With more disposable income than at any other time in the history of the world, we are well on our way to poverty—unless we change our course.

LIVE WITHIN YOUR MEANS

What would it take for you to become financially free? The obvious answer is, of course, to get out of debt. Just as obvious are the roadblocks—real and perceived—that prevent many of us from doing that. How many of these statements would you affirm, if you were honest about your financial habits?

- It takes too much time to track expenses.
- I don't really want to change my habits.

- I enjoy living beyond my means.
- Using credit cards is easier than maintaining a budget.
- My spouse and I fight when we try to budget.

While teaching basic budgeting is outside the scope of this book, hundreds of resources are available online and in bookstores that can help you overcome these common obstacles, create and maintain a budget, and keep your relationships intact.

The best way to become financially free is to commit to this simple principle—Do not buy what you cannot afford.

A late-night comedy show recently performed a sketch of this concept. It depicted a husband and wife bemoaning their credit-card debt. Suddenly, the

> *It is one of the most beautiful compensations of this life that no man can sincerely try to help another without helping himself.*
>
> —Ralph Waldo Emerson

author of a fictitious one-page book titled *Don't Buy Stuff You Cannot Afford* shows up in their kitchen. The couple is hilariously dense when it comes to money, and they can't understand the idea of saving money to buy something. The wife opens the book and reads, "If you don't have any money, you should not buy anything." Her husband remarks, "That sounds confusing! Where would you get this 'saved' money?"

The wife chimes in, "Let's say I don't have enough money to buy something. Should I buy it anyway?"

In the context of a comedy sketch, those statements sound as silly as they are. However, many of us find ourselves thinking in those terms when it comes to curbing our spending. We're so conditioned to immediate gratification that we have trouble grasping the concept of saving. Your first step toward financial freedom will be to master the content of that imaginary book and "don't buy stuff you can't afford."

MASTER THE CYCLE OF GIVING

The path to financial freedom begins with moving out of debt, and it leads to what you might consider an unlikely place—generosity. You can have it all—*if* you'll give it all away. Learning to give is an essential element of a TQL. I'm not suggesting you empty your pockets at a city park or throw dollar bills from your office window. Yet those whose lives reflect total quality, practice purposeful, effective giving.

Effective giving has four stages: trust, commitment, delight, and rest.[10]

TRUE WISDOM: SOLOMON

When God asked Solomon what he would want if he could have anything, the King of Israel asked for wisdom rather than riches. In the end, he gained both wisdom and wealth.

We're told Solomon built the temple, erected a huge palace for himself that took fourteen years to build, and organized major building programs in cities throughout Israel. He also created new cities for his cavalry, housing 1,400 chariots, 12,000 horsemen, and 4,000 stalls for horses.

Since there was no good port for trade with Egypt and the Hittites, he built a harbor on the Gulf of Akabah on the Red Sea. With this, Solomon built up unprecedented wealth by trading with his neighbors.

Solomon's choice demonstrates that with wisdom often come both administrative skill and wealth.

STAGE ONE: TRUST

You and I work hard to earn a living, and we appreciate receiving our paychecks on payday. However, we also must acknowledge we are not the source of every good thing that comes to us. We don't control the weather, the actions of others, or the global economy. Ultimately, we rely on God, who provides the health and strength that enable us to work.

We've all had the experience of receiving an unexpected gift—one we didn't earn. How have you responded to gifts like that? Those who live the TQL

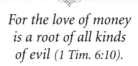

For the love of money is a root of all kinds of evil (1 Tim. 6:10).

respond by giving in return. They understand there really is more to life than money. In his book *The Automatic Millionaire* David Bach wrote, "Although you should give simply for the sake of giving, the reality is that abundance tends to flow back to those who give."[11] Those who live the TQL know this, and they hold their resources loosely, realizing they don't have total control of them and that there is enough to go around.

They also understand the laws of the harvest. Every farmer knows the laws of harvesting crops. He never anticipates harvesting corn when he's planted wheat; he never expects to plant today and harvest tomorrow; and he never expects to harvest less than he planted. The same principles apply to financial and other resources.

We Always Reap What We Sow. The person who puts time and effort into a presentation can expect a productive meeting. The student who studies for a test can expect to pass. The individual who gives before he's asked, gives generously, and gives often, can expect to receive in the same way. We reap what we sow.

We Always Reap after We Sow. No one expects a baseball player to score a run before he hits the ball. We don't expect a supervisor to praise an employee who's only started on the job that morning. Likewise, we can't expect to be rewarded financially before we give anything. That, by the way, is a common thought pattern. "I'll wait to give until I have extra." When was the last time you had extra? It seems we always need something for ourselves whenever any extra happens to come along, so don't wait to start giving until you have more than you need.

> *Life expectancy would grow by leaps and bounds if green vegetables smelled as good as bacon.*
>
> —Doug Larson

A story is told about a man who was hiking through the mountains. Having run out of water several hours before, he was relieved to come across an old-fashioned pump. As he reached for the attached cup he noticed a note hanging from the handle. Here's what it said:

> It is safe to drink from this well. I fixed the pump and put a new sucker washer in it. The washer dries out and needs to be primed. Under the large white rock west of the well is a bottle of water. There's enough water in it to prime the pump, but not enough if you take a drink first. Pour a little of the water into the pump to soak the leather washer. Then pour in the rest and pump fast. You'll soon get water. Have faith. This well won't run dry. After you've pumped all the water you want, fill

the bottle back up and put it where you found it. Put this note back in the cup, and tie the cup to the handle. Another thirsty traveler will soon be along.[12]

If you hope to receive, you must first learn to give. You will reap after you sow, but not before.

We Always Reap More Than We Sow. No farmer would ever plant a crop that yielded the same number of vegetables as the number of seeds he sowed. A typical tomato plant yields about twenty pounds of tomatoes.[13] Planting about two pounds of the flageolet bean can easily yield more than a hundred pounds of seed.[14] Again, the same is true of financial giving. My wife and I have seen this principle work in our lives time and time again. Once we felt compelled to give a thousand dollars to a cause we believed in. The following week we received a check for more than fourteen hundred dollars. I'm not promising you will always see that kind of immediate application of the law of the harvest, but I assure you the principle holds true. When you give generously to others, you can expect to receive abundant generosity yourself.

What's the first step in this kind of victorious giving? It is trust. You must believe there is greater power in being generous than in hoarding your resources. A total quality outlook on finances begins with trust.

Stage Two: Commitment

The second stage in the cycle of giving is commitment. The late comedian Jack Benny was known for portraying "the world's stingiest man." Benny once did a sketch in which he was accosted by a robber. The robber yelled, "Your money or your life!" Benny paused. The robber repeated his demand: "Look, pal, I said your money or your life." Benny fired back, "I'm thinking it over!"[15] Though we seldom have to choose between our possessions and our lives, sometimes giving can be difficult. True commitment is about surrendering our money and other resources to a higher good—without thinking it over.

Earl and Hazel Lee wrote, "Commitment is more than a sentimental decision that may change one's life for a few emotion-filled days. It is a valid act of the will, changing one's whole way of life."[16] The Lees illustrate the meaning of commitment by describing it the way an Indian dialect does: Commitment is about giving "palms down." When we drop something into someone's hand, we are unable to hold on to any part of it. Whereas when we ask a person to take something from our hand, we can still keep any part they happen to miss. In our culture, it's easy to move from enjoying our possessions to holding them tightly and grabbing for more, which is materialism.

A.W. Tozer wrote, "One of the world's worst tragedies is that we allow our hearts to shrink until there is room in them for little beside ourselves."[17] Materialism is a dangerous attitude because it keeps our focus on what we have rather than who we are and who we're becoming. It allows us to be falsely satisfied—we think that because we have lots of things we must be good people. While there's nothing wrong with driving a nice car, dressing well, and enjoying the benefits of the latest technology, when our possessions possess us and our valuables become more important than our values, we get into trouble.

GOD OWNS MY BUSINESS: STANLEY TAM

At age twenty Stanley Tam read that photographic film contained silver and that sixteen tons of the metal was washed down the drain every day in photo developing labs. The enterprising young man built a silver recovery device that could be used at photographic and x-rays labs, but no one seemed interested in his offer to split the recovered silver profits fifty-fifty.

After investing heavily in the recovery units, his savings was down to thirty-seven dollars.

Tam desperately prayed, "God, if you'll take the business and make it succeed, I will honor you in any way I possibly can." So, he set up his "factory" in his spare bedroom—and the business became a success. Obeying his commitment to honor God, he had lawyers set up the company so God was listed as senior partner with 51 percent of the profit going to church and missionary work.

Later, Tam realized that Christ on the cross had given His all, so this remarkable businessman turned 100 percent over to God and went on to write a book, *God Owns My Business*. Tam's Total Quality Life proves that there is no disconnect between faith and financial freedom.

Refuse to Be Distracted. Avoiding (or escaping) materialism requires that we do not allow ourselves to be distracted from our goal of living a TQL. Focusing on material things divides both our attention and our allegiance. One of the rulers of ancient Israel, King Hezekiah, committed himself completely to ruling wisely, obeying the laws of God, and working wholeheartedly. The record states that because of the king's commitment, he prospered. When he gave, he got; conversely, when he got, he gave.

Cultivate Contentment. My friend Jeff is fascinated by technology. He loves cameras and stereo equipment. Jeff knows his interests could become obsessions, so he's careful about how much time he spends looking at new equipment. He's so conscious of overspending in this area that he'll even shop at garage sales for new speakers. He fosters contentment by enjoying what he has and living within his means. He also works to keep an eternal perspective. Jeff uses his equipment for the benefit of others, taking photos that show the beauty of creation, for example, and recording his teenage son's original music to spend time with him and to build up his son.

Commit to an Eternal Plan. Most of us don't float around every day thinking about heaven. Our lives are filled with daily tasks and responsibilities: going to work, interacting with our loved ones, meeting the needs of our families, and taking care of ourselves.

> *Money never made a man happy yet, nor will it. The more a man has, the more he wants. Instead of filling a vacuum, it makes one.*
>
> —Benjamin Franklin

Still, within our typical days, we need to find an atypical perspective. Some call it leaving a legacy, making an impact, or changing the world. We must choose to use our resources to make a positive difference in others. When we do so, we'll find our entire outlook changes. We anticipate giving, we watch for ways we can meet needs, we go out of our way to help, and we experience delight that comes from seeing beyond ourselves and purposely contributing to the lives of those around us. Focusing on the ultimate long-term investment—eternity—keeps our finances on track here and now. Making the commitment to give, even when we'd rather do otherwise, moves our financial life to a higher level.

RESOURCES

STAGE THREE: DELIGHT

My friend Steve Weber likes to say, "If you want to change what you're getting, change what you're giving." In other words, generosity breeds generosity. As we freely give of our resources, others will do the same. I've never heard anyone express regret at having given of his or her time, talent, and financial resources. Why? Because God, who both commanded and modeled giving, rewards the practice—often in ways we didn't anticipate. That's why the third stage of victorious giving is delight. When you take delight in giving to others, you free yourself financially.

Giving is a delight and reflects a deliberate attitude of the heart. Webster's dictionary defines *delight* as "a high degree of satisfaction; joy; something that gives great pleasure."

Have you ever given a gift to a stingy person? If so, you know it's not particularly rewarding. Perhaps you've heard the classic story of the tight-fisted husband who kept all the family money in a jar in the closet. On his deathbed, he gave his wife instructions to put his money into his casket. Following his demise, the wife—who had sacrificed all her married life because of her husband's stingy approach to money—took the money from the jar and deposited it into her checking account. Then, in an appropriate response to his request, she wrote a check for the entire amount that was in the jar and put it into the casket of her dearly departed.[18]

God didn't give us his treasures so we would store them in a jar in the closet or some safety deposit box deep in a vault. He gave to us so we would give to others. He begins the cycle and expects us to complete it. The Bible says, "Every good and perfect gift is from above, coming down from the Father of the heavenly lights, who does not change like shifting shadows."[19]

God gives from a heart of unceasing love, and those who love him in return will reflect that same spirit. The words of hymn writer John Newton, notorious as a slave trader who was divinely forgiven, say it best:

> Amazing grace! How sweet the sound
> That saved a wretch like me!
> I once was lost but now am found;
> Was blind but now I see.

Newton's words of gratitude have become a gift not only to God but to the world.

Sometimes we say a person who has set a standard for quality in a given endeavor has "raised the bar." When we give, receive, and give again, we raise the bar on giving for those around us. God, of course, established the standard, but he expects us to live up to it by giving the same way he has: sacrificially, purposefully, lovingly, and gladly. When we give in this way (lightening the heavy load of another) our spirits are refreshed, our hearts our encouraged, and our faith is strengthened.

Billy Graham illustrated the concept of "pipeline giving" at a crusade in Oklahoma City some years back. He said, "God has given us two hands—one to receive with and the other to give with. We are not cisterns made for hoarding; we are channels made for sharing."[20] As we receive God's gifts and blessings with gratitude, we pour them out onto others, and receive yet again. Those who have made a commitment to giving to others will soon enter this stage of giving, in which they find delight in blessing others.

STAGE FOUR: REST

The final stage in the cycle of giving is rest. Resting in giving doesn't mean sitting still and waiting for the blessings to pile up. For our purposes resting is active. It means seeking and enjoying the rewards of a generous lifestyle. The rewards may not always be financial in nature, but the person who's pursuing a TQL is looking for good things everywhere. Did you receive a sloppy kiss from a small child (or a large animal) this morning? Did someone say thank you for a job well done? Did the moon fill your bedroom with soft light last night? Or, if you're a career person, perhaps you'll find enjoyment in having something to offer to help a new person along at work. Taking the time to help educate a subordinate not only boosts that person up the ladder and makes you feel like a hero, you just might learn something in the process.

> *Gain all you can;*
> *save all you can;*
> *give all you can.*
>
> —John Wesley

Service. Offering the gift of service can be tricky for those who struggle with saying no and ordering priorities. However, consider leading your department in a service project. If you're the boss, take your department to the downtown homeless shelter for the afternoon or "adopt a highway" and clean up litter in your town. At home offer to baby-sit your wife's friend's kids, as well as your own, so the women can have a night out together. Cook your husband's favorite meal (or take him to his favorite restaurant). Volunteer at your kids' school. Giving the gift of service is a great way to model generosity, especially to children.

Listening. People pay therapists hundreds of dollars for a fifty-minute hour just to have someone to listen to them. I'm not suggesting you open your door to the emotionally troubled, but consider instituting a certain amount of time each day or week for people to come into your office to talk about whatever is on their mind. Sometimes people hesitate to share great ideas or pressing concerns because there's no forum for simply listening. All of us want to know we're being heard, especially by our bosses or spouses. Setting aside an appropriate amount of time to listen is a gift everyone appreciates.

YOU CAN HAVE IT ALL

Experiencing TQL in your finances is counterintuitive. You'd think that having it all depends on *gaining* more for yourself. In fact, it's just the opposite. Do you remember the theme of this chapter? You can have it all—*if* you'll give it all away. Finding joy in life comes most often by blessing others, not by seeking to be blessed ourselves.

This principle is illustrated by a statement made years ago by Jim Elliot, the martyred missionary whose story is told in the motion picture *The End of the Spear*. Elliot, along with several others, gave his life to share God's love with a tribe in Ecuador. His sacrifice resulted in thousands of young adults committing their lives to serve God. Before going to Ecuador, Elliot had written these words in his journal: "He is no fool who gives what he cannot keep to gain what he cannot lose."

That is the Total Quality Life—giving yourself fully to something greater than yourself—and that is the path to true satisfaction. Try it and see.

STEPS TO TOTAL QUALITY

Take these five actions to solidify your resolve to pursue TQL.

1. If you are not using a budget, begin tracking your income and spending each month. Be sure to account for *every* item, no matter how small.

2. Review your income and expenditures for the month. Identify items that seem to be out of control.

3. Create (or review) a budget that translates your life goals into a financial plan. If you have significant debt or have had trouble sticking with a personal budget, consider seeing a financial counselor.

4. Spend time reflecting on this question: "Do I trust God enough to be generous with others?"

5. Review your giving to church, charity, and others. Identify a financial gift you can make that will stretch your ability to trust God.

6

SPIRIT

TOTAL QUALITY FAITH

You are an integrated person, a whole human being.
Therefore, to experience the Total Quality Life,
you must feed your spirit as well as your body and mind.

Kevin takes care of his body religiously, eating a healthy diet and running three to four miles every morning. Over the past year, however, Kevin grew more and more tired. He would often take naps during the day and had difficulty concentrating on his work. He assumed he was getting older and needed to slow down. Then a few months ago, Kevin discovered he needed quadruple bypass surgery. From the outside it appeared that Kevin was in perfect health. The experience taught him the importance of applying total quality to the unseen areas of life as well.

Likewise, in our efforts to create a Total Quality Life, we may understand the concepts, determine to make changes, take care of our bodies, and give generously, but if we neglect our hearts—our spiritual lives—we won't experience true TQL. Our spiritual lives affect every other aspect of our existence.

The quote attributed to seventeenth-century mathematician and philosopher Blaise Pascal is still true today: "There is a God-shaped vacuum in the heart of every man which cannot be filled by any created thing, but only by God the Creator." Because that is true, focusing on only our bodies or our careers

You don't have a soul.
You are a Soul.
You have a body.

—C. S. Lewis

will not bring fulfillment. Even the Tin Woodman in L. Frank Baum's classic book *The Wonderful Wizard of Oz* knew the heart was more important than brains or any other aspect of being. Baum masterfully demonstrates that fact in an exchange between the Tin Woodman and the Scarecrow.

"My head is stuffed with straw, you know" the Scarecrow said, "and that is why I am going to Oz to ask him for some brains."

"Oh, I see," said the Tin Woodman. "But, after all, brains are not the best things in the world."

"Have you any?" inquired the Scarecrow.

"No, my head is quite empty," answered the Woodman; "but once I had brains, and a heart also; so, having tried them both, I should much rather have a heart."

The Tin Woodman proceeds to tell the Scarecrow how he loved a Munchkin girl who wouldn't marry him until he built her a house. The wicked witch was jealous and enchanted his axe so that it slipped when he chopped wood. He progressively cut off all his limbs, which were replaced with tin by a skilled tinsmith. Furious, the witch enchanted the axe once again so that it split the Woodman in half.

> "Once more the tinner came to my help and made me a body of tin, fastening my tin arms and legs and head to it, by means of joints, so that I could move around as well as ever. But, alas! I had now no heart, so that I lost all my love for the Munchkin girl, and did not care whether I married her or not. . . ."
>
> "All the same," said the Scarecrow, "I shall ask for brains instead of a heart; for a fool would not know what to do with a heart if he had one."
>
> "I shall take the heart," returned the Tin Woodman; "for brains do not make one happy, and happiness is the best thing in the world."[1]

Frank Baum was right: the heart, or spirit, is the center of our being, and when we choose to ignore it and use only our brains (our own efforts, thoughts, strength, and resources) we become as tin men.

Most of us understand how to care for our bodies, even if we're not diligent in doing it. We need rest, a proper diet, and exercise. But how do we care for our souls?

Do not be anxious about anything, but in everything, by prayer and petition, with thanksgiving, present your requests to God (Phil. 4:6).

What are the habits and activities that make for a quality spiritual life? Let's consider three key ways to feed your spirit.

PRAYER

When I was a child, we used to sing a little song in church:

> Whisper a prayer in the morning;
> Whisper a prayer at noon;
> Whisper a prayer in the evening;
> To keep your heart in tune.

While it may sound simplistic, the formula does work. Prayer is communication between God the Father and his children. It's a way for us to bring our cares and concerns to One who is bigger than all of them, One who sees the broad picture of humanity. This great God, the Creator of all that exists, cares personally about you and me. The Bible says God sees even a sparrow who falls from a tree. He cares about even the smallest details of our lives, and prayer is the way he has provided for us to bring issues, big and small, to him for guidance and comfort.

MAN OF PRAYER: KING DAVID

David, Israel's second king, is often referred to as a warrior poet, but more accurately he was a prayer warrior. The titles of seventy-three psalms name David as author. Although written in Hebrew poetic form, they are more than mere poetry; they are passionate prayers praising God ("O Lord, our Lord, how majestic is your name in all the earth!") as well as questioning Him ("How long, O Lord? Will you forget me forever? How long will you hide your face from me?").

In David's passion for worship, the king became "a man after God's own heart."

We may feel inadequate to approach our Heavenly Father. But the key word here is *Father*. If you are a parent, you know you would be heartbroken to learn your child didn't want to talk with you because he or she felt inadequate or unworthy. Just as you want your child to approach you and talk about the day's events or whatever issue or crisis is at hand, so our Father in heaven wants us to approach him.

"Prayer brings the power of God to bear on the situations we are concerned about. Prayer is one of the ways God is able to work in our lives and in the lives of others, and it opens new possibilities. So we can freely bring all of our concerns, our thoughts and desires, our hurts and our needs to him, knowing that He is our loving Father, who wants to hear from us."[2]

Perhaps you're new to prayer and aren't sure how to begin. There's a simple acronym that can help you get started: ACTS.

Adoration. Start your prayer by acknowledging how great God is. Recognize that he is all-powerful, all-knowing, good, kind, and loving. Tell him you love him for who he is.

Confession. Confessing is acknowledging we don't always do what pleases God. When we confess, we agree with God's assessment that not every attitude and behavior in our lives measures up to his high standard. We clear the air between God and us. It's difficult to have a conversation with a friend when you know you've offended your friend in some way. In the same way, it's important to keep your relationship with God on good terms.

Thanksgiving. We'll talk more about thanksgiving in the next section of this chapter, but for now, know that expressing gratitude for both spiritual and material gifts and blessings is an essential part of prayer. When you pray, thank God for the good things he has provided in the world and for you personally.

Supplication. *Supplication* is an old-fashioned word that means to "ask humbly and earnestly." This is the part of prayer where we make requests of God. We present our needs and the needs of others to him and ask for his intervention and guidance. Although your circumstances may be difficult or uncertain, it is reassuring to know God can supply whatever you need.

Though it doesn't fit into our acronym, take the time to listen to God as well as talk to him. When you have a conversation with a friend, you don't just blurt out everything you want to say and walk away. You talk for a bit and then listen for a bit. You'll want to do the same when you pray. God wants to teach you and encourage you, but you need to give him opportunity to speak. This takes a little practice because we're so used to having chatter in our lives. Be still and listen for God's voice.

Set aside time each day for prayer, even if it's only a few moments. And remember prayer is an activity you can engage in nearly anytime—while driving, waiting between appointments, or just before going to bed at night. As the little song says, a whispered prayer at anytime of the day will keep your heart "in tune."

THANKSGIVING

Expressing thanks is not simply a part of prayer. It is a heart habit that benefits nearly every relationship. Scientists are just beginning to understand the mental and physical health benefits of being grateful. Two psychologists, Dr. Michael McCollough, of Southern Methodist University, and Dr. Robert Emmons, of the University of California at Davis, conducted the Research Project on Gratitude and Thanksgiving and found gratitude plays a significant role in a person's sense of well-being.

The study indicated that those who engaged in daily gratitude exercises reported higher levels of alertness, enthusiasm, determination, optimism, and energy. Additionally, the gratitude group experienced less depression and stress, was more likely to help others, exercised more regularly and made more progress toward personal goals.

> *The value of consistent prayer is not that He will hear us, but that we will hear Him.*
>
> —William McGill

According to the findings, people who feel grateful are also more likely to feel loved. McCollough and Emmons also noted that gratitude encouraged a positive cycle of reciprocal kindness among people since one act of gratitude encourages another.[3]

Other studies have shown that grateful people tend to be less materialistic, feel their lives are generally good, and appreciate the interconnectedness of all life.[4]

So how can we best incorporate thanksgiving, gratitude, into our days? Brother David Steindl-Rast has a simple, albeit not easy, three-step process that can help.

1. Wake Up. Steindl-Rast suggests we "wake up" to surprise. "As long as nothing surprises us," he writes, "we walk through life in a daze. Ask yourself at least twice a day, 'Isn't this surprising?' and you will soon be more awake to the surprising world in which we live." Be alert to the good things that are happening around you.

2. Be Aware. We need to be aware of the opportunities for gratitude that surround us each day—"sounds, smells, tastes, texture, colors, and, with still deeper joy, friendliness, kindness, patience, faithfulness, honesty, and all those gifts that soften the soil of our heart like warm spring rain. The more we practice awareness of the countless opportunities to simply enjoy, the easier it becomes to recognize difficult or painful experiences as opportunities, as gifts."

3. Respond Alertly. Once being awake and aware become habits, we will be quick to respond. "When a sudden rain shower is no longer just an inconvenience but a surprise gift, you will spontaneously rise to the opportunity for enjoyment. You will enjoy it as much as you did in your kindergarten days, even if you are no longer trying to catch raindrops in your wide-open mouth."[5]

Being awake, aware, and alert is the best way to cultivate gratitude in your life. But once it's part of your thinking, how can you make it part of your behavior? Here are a few things you can do right now.

- Offer a word of courage to a fearful person.
- Thank a person who's provided a service.
- Praise your spouse for supporting your career.
- Give a coworker kudos for an idea that spurred others to more innovative thinking.
- Let a coworker's boss know how the person went above and beyond on a recent project.
- Take the time to really look at your child's drawing or homework. Praise your child for creativity, neatness, thoroughness—anything that lets the child know you

admire him or her. (Throwing in a hug wouldn't hurt either.)

- Thank your assistant for consistently making you look good.
- Thank your parents for instilling a particular value in you.

Undoubtedly this list has prompted you to think of many other opportunities. All that's left is to take advantage of them.

MEDITATION

Meditation is another great way to feed your heart. I'm not talking about anything mysterious. Simply, meditation is quieting the mind and choosing a particular focus. You may focus on a particular inspirational reading, on an upcoming event at which you hope to perform well, such as a meeting or athletic

EXTREME FAITH: GEORGE MULLER

One of the most famous stories of George Muller's faith and prayer life takes place at his orphanage in Bristol, England, during the 1800s. The cupboards were bare, but Muller had the 2000 children sit down for lunch and say grace for the food he was sure was coming. Sure enough, a knock at the door announced the arrival of a shipment of donated food.

Muller determined that rather than engaging in fundraising campaigns to fund the orphanage, he would let only God know of his needs. Soon donations began arriving that would total nearly a million and a half British pounds or seven million American dollars.

During the fifty-one years Muller managed the orphanage, not one meal passed without food—even if it arrived at the last minute.

endeavor, or on an element of creation such as a leaf or flower. You meditate by relaxing yourself, opening your mind, and contemplating whatever focus you have chosen.

Meditation is good for more than your spirit. It has also been shown to lower blood pressure, improve exercise performance in people with angina, help people with asthma breathe easier, relieve insomnia and generally relax the everyday stresses of life.[6]

TWO TYPES OF MEDITATION

There are two basic types of meditation: *concentrative meditation* and *mindfulness*.

Concentrative meditation focuses attention on the breath to still the mind. Meditation practitioners believe there is a direct correlation between one's breath and one's state of the mind. For example, when a person is anxious, frightened, agitated, or distracted, the breath will tend to be shallow, rapid, and uneven. But when the mind is calm, focused, and composed, the breath will tend to be slow, deep, and regular. Focusing the mind on the continuous rhythm of inhalation and exhalation provides a natural object of meditation. As you focus your awareness on the breath, your mind becomes absorbed in the rhythm of inhalation and exhalation. As a result, your breathing will become slower and deeper, and the mind becomes more tranquil and aware.[7]

> *We have to pray with our eyes on God, not on the difficulties.*
>
> —Oswald Chambers

Mindfulness involves sitting still and simply witnessing what goes through the mind. It "can be likened to a wide-angle lens. Instead of narrowing your sight to a selected field of vision as in concentrative meditation, here you will be aware of the entire field."[8]

The Bible also mentions meditation. King David, writer of many of the psalms, was a proponent of meditation:

"Within your temple, O God, we meditate on your unfailing love" (Ps. 48:9).

"I will meditate on all your works and consider all your mighty deeds" (Ps. 77:12).

"I have more insight than all my teachers, for I meditate on your statutes" (Ps. 119:99).

"My eyes stay open through the watches of the night, that I may meditate on your promises" (Ps. 119:148).

"I remember the days of long ago; I meditate on all your works and consider what your hands have done" (Ps. 143:5).

For David, meditation meant clearing his mind of the day's cares and focusing on God's commands, characteristics, works, and promises to get a clear perspective on what was important and what was required of him as a king and as an individual.

PRACTICING MEDITATION

Like prayer, meditation may seem intimidating at first. Here are some simple steps that will help you begin practicing meditation right away.

- Find a relatively quiet place where you won't be disturbed.
- Turn off any music, TV, computer—anything that might distract you.

- Sit in a relaxed position.
- Keep your eyes open. (Closing them tends to put the body into sleep mode.)
- Pray, asking God to guard your mind and show you the truth he has for you.
- Read a short passage of the Bible or some other inspirational material.
- Think about the words, what they mean, and what they mean to you.
- Continue meditating for about fifteen minutes or so.
- Over time, build up to an hour if you can. Meditation can be of great benefit spiritually, physically, mentally, and emotionally, but it's not something you can rush. Try it several times before you decide it isn't for you. You just might be surprised at the benefits you receive.

PASCAL'S WAGER

Let's return for a moment to mathematician and philosopher Blaise Pascal. Pascal formulated an idea that has come to be known as Pascal's Wager. He wrote that it is always better to "bet" that God exists "because the expected value to be gained from believing God exists is always greater than the expected value resulting from nonbelief."[9] If God doesn't exist and we've lived to please him, we've lost nothing. Yet if he does exist, and we've lived only to please ourselves, we've lost everything. Consider the state of your heart and ask yourself where you've placed your confidence.

STEPS TO TOTAL QUALITY

Take these five actions to solidify your resolve to pursue TQL.

1. Create a spiritual timeline of your life. Identify significant spiritual moments or turning points.
2. Honestly assess your current relationship with God. Determine one way that you can improve that relationship.
3. Pray every day for two weeks using the ACTS method described in this chapter.
4. List three people to whom you are grateful for something. Within the next three days, express your thanks to each of the three.
5. Practice meditation as described in this chapter on at least two occasions in the next thirty days.

EXPERIENCING
TOTAL QUALITY

Knowing alteration is required is not enough.
You must act.

Your life transformation will be powered by—
Discipline
Change
Achievement

7

DISCIPLINE

DAILY DECISIONS THAT
REINFORCE QUALITY

Your daily actions determine the course of your life
as surely as the moon determines the tides. You must
discipline your behavior to achieve a life of quality.

When you hear the word *discipline*, what comes to
mind? Do you get a mental picture of an Ichabod
Crane-type schoolmaster asking a child to hold out his
hand to be smacked with a ruler? How about a stern
father asking his son to go out and cut a "switch"? Or
perhaps your concept is more academic; you think of the
disciplines of philosophy, mathematics, or psychology.
Maybe you even think, "If I had more discipline, I could lose
a few pounds." To most people, discipline has a negative con-
notation.

You might be surprised to know the dictionary also
defines discipline as "training that corrects, molds, or perfects
the mental faculties or moral character."[1] There's nothing
there about schoolmasters or switches. For our purposes,
discipline means *training*. To be disciplined is to train yourself

to think and behave in a way that reinforces your decision to pursue the Total Quality Life.

Part of a TQL is living in freedom mentally, emotionally, spiritually, and physically. Certain practical behaviors go along with that. Auditing your beliefs and determining your values frees your mind. Associating with positive people and choosing laughter over sadness frees your soul. Reducing clutter and maximizing your minutes frees your body. Gaining financial freedom and leaving a legacy frees your spirit. When we train ourselves to do these things each day, they work together to form the foundation of a quality life by enabling us to focus on what's truly important to us.

> *Discipline is remembering what you want.*
>
> —David Campbell

As you can see, there's no need to be nervous about the word *discipline*. So let's move ahead and take a closer look at one of the disciplines of TQL.

AUDIT YOUR BELIEFS

An audit is a methodical examination and review. To make significant changes in your life, to stride rather than wander toward a TQL, you need to know what you believe about the most important things in your life: faith, spouse, relationships, career, and future. You need to audit those beliefs; that is, you need to review them. I know it seems obvious, but in case you've never thought of it this way, let me just say you can't change your beliefs if you don't know what they are.

Below you'll find a set of prompts to help you articulate your beliefs for each category. This isn't a feel-good, pop-psychology exercise. Neither is it comprehensive. It is a springboard to get you thinking on a deeper level about where you are and where you hope to be. Take your time with it; you may be surprised by what you learn about yourself.

FAITH

Do you have faith in someone or something other than yourself? If so, what or whom?

What are your top five nonnegotiable faith-related beliefs?

Does your faith impact your daily decisions? How?

Does your faith determine your moral code of behavior? If so, what are the main points of your moral code?

SPOUSE

If you are married, what value do you place on your marriage?

Do you love your spouse? If so, how do you show it?

Do you respect your spouse? If so, how do you show it?

Do you believe your spouse loves and respects you? If so, how does he or she demonstrate that?

How do you contribute to the quality of your marriage?

If you aren't married, is marriage something you intend or wish to pursue in the future? Why or why not?

RELATIONSHIPS

How important are your relationships with people other than your immediate family?

Which relationships are most important to you? Why?

Are the majority of your relationships long-term or short-term?

How do your relationships typically end?

How do you contribute to the quality of your relationships?

CAREER

What is the value of your career?

Describe the course of your career.

Did you choose it? If not, who did? Why?

Are you fulfilled in your career? Are you impacting those around you in a significant way?

How do you contribute to the quality of your career?

What do you hope to gain from your career in the future?

FUTURE

Do you place greatest value on your past, your present, or your future?

Describe your ideal future. What will your life be like in ten years if nothing changes? What changes do you hope to achieve?

How different are your two visions?

How do you contribute to the expected quality of your future?

Do you believe the future can be better than either the past or the present?

This exercise isn't intended to help you write your life story. It is meant to help you establish a mental and emotional starting point for your TQL. Knowing what you believe and how you act out those beliefs will help you understand how and where you need to change.

Keeping the Faith: Joseph

The Old Testament's Joseph had a dream of becoming a great leader, one who would save his people. While the dream was noble, the dreamer was a brash bragger—until his brothers sold him as a slave into Egypt. Eventually thrown into an Egyptian prison, Joseph discovered God's gifts are never wasted. Even there his management skills were recognized.

Later Joseph was promoted to prime minister and placed in charge of food distribution during a seven-year famine. When his brothers went to Egypt for grain, they were met by none other than the brother they had sold into slavery.

God will use life's adversities to refine us into the leaders or managers who honor Him.

Beliefs are closely linked to values, so let's move ahead and explore your values and how they affect your life.

DETERMINE YOUR VALUES

I like this definition of values: "Values are our subjective reactions to the world around us. They guide and mold our options and behavior."[2] Typically values are not formed by what people tell us, rather how they behave toward us and how we observe them behaving toward others. "Values tell us what we should believe, regardless of any evidence or lack thereof."[3]

Values are the intermediaries between your beliefs and your actions. They are the guiding principles that shape the course of your life. Take a look at the list below to help identify your values. Circle all of those that are important to you.

Accomplishment
Accountability
Accuracy
Adventure
Beauty
Challenge
Change
Cleanliness
Collaboration
Commitment
Communication
Community
Competence
Competition
Concern for others
Content over form
Continuous improvement
Cooperation
Creativity
Customer satisfaction
Decisiveness
Democracy
Discipline
Discovery
Efficiency
Equality
Excellence
Fairness
Faith
Family
Freedom

Friendship
Fun
Global view
Good will
Goodness
Gratitude
Hard work
Harmony
Honesty
Honor
Independence
Inner peace
Innovation
Integrity
Joy
Justice
Knowledge
Leadership
Love
Loyalty
Meaning
Merit
Money
Openness
Peace
Patriotism
Perfection
Personal growth
Pleasure
Positive attitude
Power
Practicality
Preservation

Privacy
Problem solving
Progress
Prosperity
Punctuality
Quality of work
Resourcefulness
Respect for others
Responsiveness
Safety
Security
Self-reliance
Service
Simplicity
Skill
Speed
Stability
Standardization
Status
Strength
Success
Systemization
Teamwork
Timeliness
Tolerance
Tradition
Tranquility
Trust
Truth
Unity
Variety
Wisdom[4]

If you're like most people, you probably identified many of the values as your own. From your long list, choose your top ten. From that list, choose your top five. Out of your top five values, which is the one most important to you?

Your top five, or maybe even your top ten, are your core values, the values that most influence your decisions and relationships. Transfer the list of your core values to your daily planner, or hang it in your office or next to your bathroom mirror—wherever you'll see it often. Keeping your values visible will help you focus on them when you're confronted with difficult decisions and choices.

ASSOCIATE WITH POSITIVE PEOPLE

Recently I saw part of a television program on which a well-known entertainer was interviewed. A young woman in the audience asked her how she had overcome the stereotypes of both her gender and her race. The entertainer said she had consciously chosen the people with whom she associated. Her group of friends wanted the same things she wanted. They wanted to stretch their creativity, to be successful, and to strive for excellence in all their endeavors. She said she knew people from her old neighborhood who were still spending their days

A cheerful heart is good medicine, but a crushed spirit dries up the bones (Prov. 17:22).

standing on street corners, never accomplishing anything. She chose not to associate with them, not because she thought she'd arrived or that she was in any way better than they were. She simply wanted to be challenged to succeed, so she chose new friends.

Likewise, the person who chooses to associate with positive people will be challenged to be positive, to see possibility where once existed only obstacle. Positive people will challenge and encourage you toward greater maturity and success.

CHOOSE LAUGHTER

Being sad, morose, melancholy, or moody won't help you meet goals or experience personal growth. However, laughter can. Besides being downright fun, laughter has health benefits. Laughter can:

- reduce stress
- reduce blood pressure
- elevate mood
- strengthen the immune system
- improve brain function
- protect the heart

Until you value yourself, you will not value your time. Until you value your time, you will not do anything with it.

—M. Scott Peck

Laughter activates the body chemistry that generates the will to live, and it increases our capacity to fight disease. Laughing relaxes the body and reduces problems associated with high blood pressure, strokes, arthritis, and ulcers. Some research suggests laughter also may reduce the risk of heart disease. Historically, research has shown that distressing emotions such as depression, anger, anxiety, and stress are related to heart disease. A study done at the University of

Maryland Medical Center suggests a good sense of humor and the ability to laugh at stressful situations helps mitigate the damaging physical effects of distressing emotions.[5]

Humor is also vital to our mental health. Here are a few reasons why:

- Humor enhances our ability to connect with others.
- Humor helps us replace distressing emotions with pleasurable feelings. We cannot feel angry, depressed, anxious, or resentful and experience humor at the same time.[6]
- Humor changes behavior—when we experience humor we talk more, make more eye contact with others, and touch others.
- Humor increases energy, and with increased energy we may perform activities that we might otherwise avoid.

According to experts, "By the time a child reaches preschool, he or she will laugh about three hundred times a day. Adults laugh an average of seventeen times a day."[7]

Why not be better than average? Laugh more!

ORGANIZE YOUR SPACE

Clutter and the kudzu vine have a lot in common. Kudzu is a vine native to Japan and China that came to the American South in the 1920s. Left to its own devices, it will cover anything in its path. I've seen photos of trees, buildings, semitrucks, fields, and signs covered by the vine. In the same way, clutter seems to grow by itself, eventually covering every available surface. Unfortunately, unlike kudzu, clutter doesn't die in the winter.

Clutter is a forbidding obstacle that obscures the road to a TQL. Here are some simple suggestions that will go a long way toward eliminating clutter from your life.

General Guidelines

- Start with the area of your life that causes you the greatest pain.
- Create a list of the areas you want to work on in order of priority.
- Include a deadline for completing each project.
- Tackle one small area at a time, such as a drawer, cabinet, or shelf.
- Set aside time each week to work on a different area.
- Move systematically through your office or home.
- Finish one area before beginning another.

People First: Fred Smith

Fred Smith got a C in a Yale economics class for an idea that the professor belittled as unworkable. That idea—to deliver time-sensitive packages overnight—eventually became FedEx.

Smith's company became the first American business to make over ten billion dollars in annual profit. Beginning with just 186 packages delivered the first night, FedEx now delivers in over two hundred countries using over 6,000 aircraft, 46,000 vehicles, and 141,000 employees.

Not only did Smith change the way packages are delivered, he changed the way corporations dealt with customers and employees by introducing the P-S-P principle: people, service, profit. Smith's daily decisions to place people first have proven that TQL can be achieved even by the busiest, most powerful leaders.

- Recruit organizing assistants, such as friends, family, or your administrative assistant.
- If no volunteers step forward, consider hiring a professional organizer to help.

SET A GOAL FOR YOUR SPACE

- Determine what you want from your space, especially storage space, before beginning. Do you want to keep and store many things? Are you interested in maximizing access to your most important items? Do you want to rid yourself of all the junk?
- Ruthlessly evaluate every storage decision you make to meet your goals.
- Determine the resources you will need (such as storage containers, calendars, or folders) before you begin the hard work of de-cluttering your space.

ASK HARD QUESTIONS OF EVERYTHING YOU OWN

- When was the last time you used it?
- When will you realistically need it again?
- Why would you need it again?
- Who might ask for it?
- Is it easily replaceable?
- What's the worst thing that would happen if you got rid of it?
- Does it enhance your TQL by being either beautiful, useful, or loved?

Let Go of Excuses

Excuse: It was expensive, and I can't stand to see it go to waste.

Reality: If you're not using it, it's already wasted.

Excuse: I might need it someday.

Reality: If you haven't used it in a year, you probably never will.

Excuse: It was a gift.

Reality: Once you receive a gift, it's yours to do with as you see fit.

Excuse: I don't have time to get organized.

Reality: You don't have time to waste looking through stacks of papers to find a phone number, receipt, or credit card statement.

Sort It Out

- Designate areas to sort items to "keep," "part with," and "discard."
- Keep the items you know you need or love.
- Part with items that may have value to someone—but not to you.
- Discard items that can be used by no one.
- Further sort your "part with" items into two groups— "donate" and "sell."
- If you're unsure whether you're ready to part with something, keep it for one more year. If you still haven't used it, get rid of it.
- Create a "needs repair" list for items missing parts or accessories.

- Box and haul your "give away" items to a worthy recipient.
- Immediately set a date when you will sell other items.
- Haul your "discard" items to the curb immediately.

FIND STORAGE SOLUTIONS

- Designate a home for everything you own—no halfway spots.
- Store like items together according to purpose, including accessories and related items.
- Store items nearest the point where you use them.
- Store items you use most often in more accessible spaces.
- Keep climate in mind, including heat, moisture, and insects.
- Leave 15 percent of your space free for future additions.
- Plan to go through your spaces to purge them once a year.[8]

MAXIMIZE YOUR MINUTES

It's so easy to think in terms of long-range planning or even daily to-do lists that we forget about the minutes. Stephen Covey's illustration of the big and little rocks is useful here. We

Don't waste your time on useless work, mere busywork, the barren pursuits of darkness (Eph. 5:11 The Message).

definitely need to plan for the big rocks (major projects) by blocking out time, but we can't lose sight of the smaller tasks that take only a few minutes and tend to pile up day to day because we think we don't have time to do them.

My solution is to "maximize the minutes" of my day. Here are six tips to help:

1. *Allot Time.* On your to-do list, make a time-allotted note next to each task. That way, when you have, say, ten minutes to spare, you can use the time to accomplish something that takes only ten minutes to do.

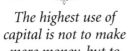

> *The highest use of capital is not to make more money, but to make money do more for the betterment of life.*
>
> —Henry Ford

2. *Work Backward.* Rather than simply setting the alarm for 7 a.m. to make a 10:30 flight, consider how long it could take to check in, find a parking space, and travel from home to the airport. Then consider what needs to be done before you can leave the house. Taking all factors into consideration when planning your day can save many minutes.

3. *Visualize Your Whole Day.* Consider what needs to be done today, but not tomorrow or next week. Make today's items Priority A—things that can't wait. Then prioritize the rest of your tasks as Priority B—things that could wait, or Priority C—things that must wait.

4. *Use a Timer.* Sometimes a one-hour lunch can slip into ninety minutes or even two hours. A five-minute phone call can morph into a twenty-minute conversation. If your minutes keep slipping away, set a timer to keep yourself accountable. There are probably timer features on your PDA, computer, watch, or cell phone. Use them. Then hold yourself accountable to keeping your time commitment.

5. *Ask, "What's Important Now?"* As you're considering whether to do what's just been placed in front of you, ask

yourself whether it is truly important. If you don't know, find out. Once you have the answer, you can determine whether it's an A-, B-, or C-level priority, rather than simply taking care of it because it's on your desk or in your inbox.

6. *Keep a Diary.* People who are trying to lose weight are often encouraged to keep food diaries, recording all they eat during the day. Try keeping a time diary, recording your use of each minute of the day. Sure, you have your planner, but how often do you really stick to it? Keep track of how you spend your time for a week, and you'll be amazed at all the minutes that are leaking out of your schedule. Use your completed diary to evaluate your use of time.

- What percentage of your time was spent productively (on building relationships and career, service, education)?
- How much was spent resting (see chapter 4)?
- How much was lost on mindless pursuits, such as excessive television watching, Internet surfing, or video games?
- Are you satisfied with how you spent your time?
- Are there ways you'd like to spend your time?

Minutes matter. You have hundreds available every day that you can waste or invest. What will you choose?

PURSUE FINANCIAL FREEDOM

Chapter 5 was all about giving and the joy that results when we give gladly and generously. But that lifestyle is impossible when the giver is in financial bondage due to a heavy personal debt load. In the wisdom literature of ancient

Israel, a wise man wrote, "The rich rules over the poor, And the borrower *becomes* the lender's slave."[9] In ancient times, that was literally true. A person who had debts could be sold to pay them. Today, that proverb is figuratively true in that a person who has a great deal of debt winds up working for the creditor by paying large sums in interest.

The more consumer debt you carry, the more difficult it is for you to get a good interest rate on a mortgage—or to get a mortgage at all. The heavier your debt, the worse your credit rating—which even affects how much you pay for your car insurance. There's no advantage to being in debt.

On the flip side, here is one unparalleled advantage to living debt free: You get to use *your* money the way *you* want to. It's yours. It doesn't belong to a bank somewhere that doesn't care if your business succeeds or if you can help pay for your parents' long-term care. When you live debt free, your money is yours. This kind of freedom is critical for living a Total Quality Life.

Jean Chatzky, editor at large for CNNMoney.com and author of *Pay it Down*, has created a straightforward, common-sense, nine-step plan to help people become financially free for good. Here are the highlights.

1. Assess the Problem. Financial struggles are like any problem: If you don't know the cause or source, treating only the symptoms won't make it better. Find out what's causing your debt.

2. Set Achievable Goals. Paying off debt can seem an insurmountable task. Breaking it down into smaller steps, however, can push it into the realm of possibility. Say you have $12,000 in credit card debt. If you can pay $700 per month, you'll be debt free in less than two years. If you're only paying $300 per month now, you'll need to figure out where to get that extra $400. Because you've already determined where your money is going in step 1, you know where you can cut back. Eating out less often, making coffee at home, switching television services, or repairing instead of replacing your car make the difference between making minimum credit card payments that stretch out for decades and paying off your debt.

Love is patient, love is kind. It does not envy, it does not boast, it is not proud. It is not rude, it is not self-seeking, it is not easily angered, it keeps no record of wrongs. Love does not delight in evil but rejoices with the truth. It always protects, always trusts, always hopes, always perseveres (1 Cor. 13:4–7).

3. Manage Your Credit Score. Your credit score may be the single most important number in your life. It determines the rate you'll receive on everything from mortgages to car insurance to lines of credit. Here are some easy ways to protect it.

- Find out what your credit score is by ordering a report at myfico.com.
- Pay on time. Timely payments make up 35 percent of your score.
- Use less of your available credit, aiming for 30 percent. Don't close cards, though. That reduces your available credit, which reduces your score.
- Don't apply for new credit cards, which will also lower your score.
- Keeping your credit cards for more than two years improves your score.

4. Track Your Spending. If you're in debt, you're living on more than you make. To turn that tide, you must know three things: what's coming in, where it's going, and where it should be going. Tracking every penny for a month will tell you if you're spending twenty dollars a month at the vending machine—that's $240 per year! Wouldn't you rather put that money toward your credit card bill? You'd be that much closer to being debt free.

5. Reduce Your Interest Rates. It's possible to negotiate lower interest rates with your credit card companies; sometimes it's simply a matter of calling and asking for them. Refinancing a home, car, or student loan also can bring huge cost benefits. It's worth your while to talk with a lender.

> *You cannot kill time without injuring eternity.*
>
> —Henry David Thoreau

6. Sell Assets. There are only two ways to reduce debt quickly: earn more or spend less. Selling assets could do both at the same time by bringing in money while reducing your obligations. Consider selling your home and moving to something less expensive. Could you sell a vehicle or other large asset? Have you considered a second job? These are drastic measures, but they may be warranted if your debt load is high.

7. Get Help if You Need It. Seeking the help of a credit counselor is not a sign of weakness. Credit counseling can help you when it feels like no matter what you do, you can't get ahead. Not all counselors are created equal, however. Make sure the counselor you choose is a member of the National Foundation of Credit Counselors or Independent Association of Credit Counselors; both require their counselors to be certified.

8. Pay Down Smartly. It's difficult to know which bills you should pay off first. As you prioritize, consider the cost of your debt. Credit cards are generally more expensive than car loans, which cost more than tax-deductible mortgages, which are more expensive than deductible student loans. Pay down your highest cost debt first.

Also, consider your credit score. To improve your credit score, pay the cards with the biggest balances relative to your credit limit rather than the ones with the highest rates. This improves your utilization ratio, which tells lenders how much of your available borrowing power you've accessed. The closer you are to your limits, the higher the perception that you will not pay on time.

Consider your cumulative minimum payments. Pay off cards with small balances as soon as possible. That will free more money to attack the larger debts.

9. Get Ahead and Stay Ahead. In the process of becoming financially free, there are a few principles that, if you follow them carefully, will keep you moving forward.

- Always pay more than is required. Minimum payments are a great way for you to stay in debt for the rest of your life. Paying even a small amount more than the minimum each month can cut years off your debt.
- Always pay on time. Late payments are rewarded by higher interest rates.
- Use debit instead of credit. Debit cards use your money. Credit cards use someone else's. Your goal is to avoid accruing new debt.

- Save something. Even when you're paying off debt, try to put something into savings. As your debt goes down and your savings goes up, you'll be less likely to need to resort to credit when emergencies arise.
- Practice patience. You know by now there's no magic formula for getting out of debt. It takes willpower and cultivating good and wise habits.[10]

You cannot experience TQL if you are a slave to debt. Financial freedom is a critical element in quality living. It also lays the foundation for leaving a lasting legacy.

YOUR LEGACY

Chuck Stecker, in his book *Men of Honor, Women of Virtue*, offers an eye-opening understanding of the concept of legacy, which he shared at a baseball game just after he and a friend watched Mark McGwire hit the first of his seventy home runs in the 1998 season.

A few moments later, as we finally settled back into our seats, the gentleman sitting next to me turned and asked me . . . , "Chuck, what do you think the legacy of Mark McGwire will be?"

I . . . replied, "I don't think that's really your question. What you are really asking is what I think the final legend of Mark McGwire will be. . . . I'm not sure about Mark McGwire's legacy because that will be determined by the quality of man he is—the fiber and fabric of which he is made. Not knowing

McGwire personally, I can't make that assessment. While it's easy to speculate about the legend—the individual records and accomplishments—it's far more difficult to determine the legacy."[11]

Leaving a legacy is all about leaving something of value—our character, our integrity—for those who come behind. The journey toward a TQL in itself is a legacy. Your family, friends, and coworkers are watching you. They're observing as you make positive changes in your life, and your example is the best legacy you could possibly leave.

Getting your house in order and reducing the confusion gives you more control over your life. Personal organization somehow releases or frees you to operate more effectively.

—Larry King

STEPS TO TOTAL QUALITY

Take these five actions to solidify your resolve to pursue TQL.

1. Undertake an audit of your beliefs as described in this chapter. Describe the person that emerges from this exercise and determine whether he or she matches your vision of TQL.
2. Review the list of values given in this chapter. Identify your five core values.
3. Assess the outlook of your closest associates. Determine how closely their beliefs and values match your vision for TQL.
4. Within the next twenty-one days, organize the space in your home or office.

5. Audit your use of time for two weeks. Determine where the minutes are leaking out of your schedule and create a plan to stop the flow.

8

CHANGE

REDESIGNING YOUR LIFE
FOR TOTAL QUALITY

No progress is possible without change.
To achieve the Total Quality Life, you must surrender
what you are for what you will become.

I f you've ever watched any of the home makeover shows, you
know how they work. The show's hosts visit a family that's
struggling for reasons of illness, unemployment, or natural disaster
and sends them on a week's vacation while a team of builders
remodels their home. Occasionally the hosts of the show even
raze the family's old home and start from scratch. When the
family returns and their new home is revealed, they are unfail-
ingly shocked to see the changes. The finished product always
exceeds their expectations.

Have you considered that the modifications you're making
might result in a life that exceeds your expectations? Wait. Do
you even know what your expectations are? Have you ever
taken the time to ask yourself what you hope to accomplish
with your life? Have you determined what you need to do,
what kind of person you need to be, to live with no regrets?

No matter your age or stage of life, it's not too late to embark on an extreme life makeover.

Let's examine some changes you may need to make to have a life of total quality. None of them is easy to achieve. Yet if you are serious about creating a Total Quality Life, you'll need to do the hard work of managing change in several important areas.

BANISH NEGATIVE THINKING

Roman emperor and philosopher Marcus Aurelius said, "The happiness of your life depends upon the quality of your thoughts; therefore, guard accordingly, and take care that you entertain no notions unsuitable to virtue and reasonable nature." I believe the emperor was correct in his assessment. Your life is only as good as you perceive it to be.

My friend Fred went through a tough time with his teenage daughter a few years ago. In therapy the daughter revealed she didn't believe her parents loved her. Fred and his wife were shocked. They adored their daughter and believed they had shown their feelings by their actions. When Fred voiced his reaction to the counselor, the counselor said, "It doesn't matter what you think you've said or done, your daughter doesn't feel loved. And what she feels and understands is what's real."

Fred and his wife struggled to grasp the concept that their daughter's perceptions were her reality, and no amount of discussion was going to change it. Once they did, however, both parents humbly asked their daughter's forgiveness for not loving her in ways she could feel and comprehend. That apology turned the tide of their daughter's rebellion and anger; and Fred, his wife, and his daughter chose to think and behave in positive ways toward each other. Today the family is functioning as a healthy family should.

In the same way, your thoughts will shape your actions. Negative thinking will prevent you from making many of the changes you'll need to pursue a Total Quality Life.

ELIMINATE ANGER AND DISCOURAGEMENT

Eliminate anger? Seriously? Yes! Of course, I'm not talking about the anger we rightly feel over injustice and wrongdoing.

The anger we need to eliminate is the anger we experience when someone cuts us off in traffic, when our spouse spends money we had allocated for bills, or when our children leave our tools out in the rain. That kind of anger is counterproductive; it detracts from the quality of our lives.

> *Make no little plans; they have no magic to stir men's blood and probably will themselves not be realized. Make big plans; aim high in hope and work, remembering that a noble, logical diagram once recorded will not die.*
>
> —Daniel H. Burnham

Do you know the root of all anger? It's simple: unmet expectations. You wouldn't get angry at the driver who cut you off if you were anticipating being cut off. You wouldn't get angry at your spouse for spending money if you weren't planning on having it available. And you wouldn't get angry at your child if you expected your child to act immaturely, as children tend to do.

EXTREME MAKEOVER: THE APOSTLE PETER

Peter was one of Christ's most outspoken disciples, but he had one problem—his foot was usually in his mouth. When Jesus warned the disciples that He will be crucified, but rise again, Peter took Him aside to say, "This shall never happen to You."

Jesus replied, "Get behind me, Satan! You are a stumbling block to me; you do not have in mind the things of God, but the things of men." But on the day of Pentecost, the Holy Spirit performed an extreme makeover on this well-intentioned loud mouth. The Spirit transformed Peter into an effective spokesman for the gospel.

Often, it is only through the Holy Spirit's power that we become the people of quality God intends us to be.

Friends of mine, John and Judy, separated and then divorced about six years ago. After four years apart, John said to Judy, "I went looking for a better Judy, and there isn't one." The two were able to work through their issues and reconcile, and they've been happily and joyously married for two years. What's the difference between what they have now and their first attempt at marriage? It is how they manage their expectations. Judy says, "We realize what we have now; we treat each other as gifts. The irritating things, the things that used to make me angry, just aren't worth damaging the relationship. We talk about any grievances right away, but as much as we're able, we most often simply choose to let them go. I never dreamed marriage could be this good."

When you find yourself getting angry, ask, "What expectation of mine wasn't met in this situation?" For example, you expected your spouse to be there when you arrived home with dinner for two, but the house was dark. This makes you angry. Instead of internally bashing your spouse's irresponsibility and lack of consideration, think back through the situation. Did he or she know you were bringing dinner home? Did you ask that your spouse be home at a certain time? Is it possible that something came up at work that made him or her late?

Being angry is usually a waste of precious time and energy. Consider giving others the benefit of the doubt, and examine your expectations before you become angry.

Discouragement is another time and energy drain. If you're feeling discouraged, you have a lack of courage or confidence, which happens to us all on occasion. Knowing it will come, prepare yourself. What fills you with courage or confidence? My friend Mary (from chapter 4) keeps the photo of herself with her marathon medal in her office. When she feels discouraged, looking at it reminds her of what she's capable of.

Maybe there's a motivational poster or saying that inspires you. Hang it where you'll see it often. Maybe you have a friend who is an especially gifted encourager. Find what works to shake off discouragement and get it in place. Then when discouragement hits, you'll be prepared to meet it head on and won't need to spend hours in the dumps trying to renew your own strength.

TRACK LIFE CHANGE IN YOUR JOURNAL

The changes you'll need to make will not be easy. You'll become discouraged sometimes and get pulled off track. But if you record your life changes in a journal, that will happen less often. Many people object to keeping a daily journal, but

I can't recommend it highly enough as a measure of your progress toward a TQL. Journaling will help you articulate your random thoughts about your life—both the exciting and the blasé. Here are a few of the key benefits of journaling:

- Journaling can be a form of meditation (for more on meditation see chapter 6).
- Journaling can provide an outlet for pent-up emotions.
- Journaling gives your ideas and dreams a place to grow and be respected.
- Journaling allows you to gain clarity as you sort through the deluge of daily life.
- Journaling can bring insight as you deal with life issues honestly and privately.
- Journaling allows you to look back and see how much progress you've made.

There is no right or wrong way to journal. But sometimes journaling can seem intimidating. A book of blank pages can bring on a severe case of writer's block. Here are a few prompts to help you fill a journal.

- Complete these sentences:
  - Today I am grateful for . . .
  - Right now, I am feeling . . .
  - One way to lighten my life would be to . . .
  - Three things I know to be true are . . .
  - I have faith that . . .
  - My life is lacking . . .

- Start with a quote that provokes thought.
  - Write about an image you saw—artwork, a photograph, a gesture observed.
  - Write about your feelings on a certain event, idea, or person.
  - Write about a change in your life and how you dealt with it.
  - List five ways an experience affected you positively.
  - Write about your ideal life.
  - Collect photos (or anything that has to do with your dream) and put them in your journal.
  - Visualizing your dreams is an effective tool for making them happen.
- Another exercise is to use your journal to answer life questions, such as:
  - What decisions brought you to where you are today?
  - Where do you want to go from here?
  - What's the hardest decision you've ever made?
  - What's the biggest breakthrough you've had recently?
  - What's the biggest challenge you've ever faced?
  - What do these experiences teach you about yourself?
  - What are your goals in the areas of career, relationships, health, or spirituality?

Write freely in your journal. Don't worry about spelling or grammar. Don't worry about smudged ink or cross-outs; your journal is for you and you alone. You may share it with someone later, but when you are writing, write it for yourself. Don't write to impress anyone. Be true to yourself. Finding time to journal regularly will accelerate the pace of your life changes.[1]

BUILD HEALTHY RELATIONSHIPS

Human beings were created to live in community. In the Bible, after God stated his whole creation was good, he observed, "It is not good for the man to be alone. I will make a helper suitable for him."[2] God knew from the beginning that people need each other. Remember that song "People" from *Funny Girl* that Barbra Streisand made popular?

> People, people who need people,
> Are the luckiest people in the world.[3]

Though the song and its context are not particularly scientific or academic, there's much truth in what they communicate. People really do need each other.

Dean Ornish, author of *Dr. Dean Ornish's Program for Reversing Heart Disease*, *Love and Survival*, and several other books, has proven through clinical research that humans need personal interaction for both emotional and physical reasons.

Think about things that are excellent and worthy of praise (Phil. 4:8 NLT).

Loneliness and isolation affect our health. They increase the likelihood that we may engage in destructive behaviors like smoking and overeating, and decrease the likelihood that we will make lifestyle choices that are life-enhancing. Loneliness and isolation also increase the likelihood of disease and premature death from all causes, and they keep us from fully experiencing the joy of everyday life.

Anything that promotes isolation often leads to illness and suffering. Anything that promotes love, intimacy, connection, and community is healing. Healing is a process of becoming whole. Even the words *heal, whole,* and *holy* come from the same root.

We are creatures of community. In our culture, the idea of spending time taking care of each other and creating communities has become increasingly rare. Ignoring these ideals imperils our survival. Awareness is the first step in healing, both individually and socially. When we understand how important these issues are, we can do something about them. Relationship building actions include:

- spending time with our friends and family
- improving communication skills
- practicing confession and forgiveness
- showing compassion, altruism, and service
- displaying affection

When we increase the love and intimacy in our lives, we also increase the health, joy, and meaning in our lives.[4]

Ornish believes positive, winning relationships enhance the quality of our lives. If that's true, there are two secrets you need to know to make the most of them.

RELATIONSHIP SECRET 1: BEFRIEND YOURSELF

The fact that you're reading this book tells me you want to improve your life. You're dissatisfied with at least a portion of it, and you want to make it better. I commend you for your perseverance. Sometimes, though, those of us who strive for improvement can be hard on ourselves. We perceive that whatever we do isn't quite enough; we could be—should be—doing more.

Perhaps. But think about your best friend for a moment. Do you impose the same unreachable standards on your friend that you do on yourself? Probably not. You love your friend for who he or she is, and you hope the person will choose to grow and mature to enjoy life more and be happier, not simply to cross an item off a to-do list and be able to say he or she has "arrived." Below are some ways you can show love to yourself. Some may seem simple or even silly, but give them a chance. If you find you're embarrassed to try them, maybe you're being a bit hard on yourself.

1. *Be Kind to Yourself.* Refuse to criticize yourself for either thoughts or behaviors. Criticism doesn't change anything.

2. *Be Patient with Yourself.* Treat yourself the way you treat others you love.

3. *Praise Yourself.* Tell yourself every day what you're doing well.

4. *Support Yourself.* When you need a hand, reach out to friends and loved ones, and let them help you.

5. *Take Care of Yourself.* Give your body the nutrition and exercise it needs.

6. *Like Yourself.* Look into your eyes and say, "I love you" every day.[5]

7. *Honor Yourself.* Make a list of things you like about yourself. Your list could contain physical traits, character qualities, values you hold, actions you've taken, anything about yourself you like. Put this list in your journal. Make a note every time someone says something nice about you. These notes will come in handy when you start to feel discouraged.

8. *Have Compassion on Yourself.* If you're judging yourself for something you said or did, think about how you'd feel if a friend did it. Would it even matter to you? If not, dismiss it. If so, deal with it.

> *To will is to select a goal, determine a course of action that will bring one to that goal, and then hold to that action 'til the goal is reached. The key is action.*
>
> —Michael Hanson

9. *Think Well of Yourself.* Counteract negative or critical thoughts. When you catch yourself thinking, "I'm so dumb; I don't know why I even bothered to open my mouth in that meeting," counteract the thought with, "I'm an intelligent, gifted person; I have valuable and creative ideas."

10. *Comfort and Nurture Yourself.* It's easy to slough off small things that make us feel great. Does a cup of tea soothe your spirit? Nine holes? Rereading your favorite novel? Don't hesitate to take the time to nurture yourself. Again, you wouldn't think less of your friend for doing so, so why not treat yourself?

11. *Affirm Yourself.* Write personal affirmations in your journal. This can feel so corny, but it helps. Every day, write something positive about yourself: "I am kind"; "I love my wife and she knows it"; "I am a hard worker"; "I have a great sense of humor." If you can, say them out loud. If you can't, read them until you believe them.

12. *Let Others Affirm You.* Ask a couple of people you trust to give you a list of things they like about you. Make sure they know it doesn't have to be comprehensive—just a few things will do. Then when you lapse into discouragement or negativity, look at the list and remember you're loved and appreciated.[6]

RELATIONSHIP SECRET 2: BEFRIEND OTHERS

Solomon, the wisest man who ever lived, wrote, "A man who has friends must himself be friendly."[7] When she was a young girl, one of my friends used to open her front door in the summer and play the piano loudly, hoping a famous pianist she admired would happen to stroll by and discover her. Not surprisingly, it never happened. Of course, living in the rural Midwest didn't exactly help her chances.

*O Lord, my Rock
and my Redeemer
(Ps. 19:14).*

Sitting around waiting for relationships to fall into your lap is not the way to get them. It simply won't happen. And that's not true just for new ones. Waiting for your friend or relative to renew a relationship with you is a sure way to keep your distance. Remember that saying "If it's to be, it's up to me"? That's how relationships work. You must make the first move. Even if your brother-in-law owes you a phone call, call him. Even if your friend in another state said she'd e-mail you as soon as she got settled in her new place, contact her. Relationships renew us, revitalize us, and motivate us.

CREATE A STRATEGIC PLAN

To implement the changes you need to make in pursuing your TQL, you must work from a strategic plan. It's not enough to say you want to do things differently or better. You must specify exactly which things, how much better, when you'll do them, and why.

W. Edwards Deming, whose principles we discussed in chapter 2, developed what's known as the Deming cycle, or PDCA (Plan-Do-Check-Act).[8] Let's consider it as a template for creating a strategic life plan.

PDCA

PDCA is a model for implementing change. As you can see from the diagram below, it's circular rather than linear; so, like the TQL, this tool is a process and a way to experience continuous improvement.

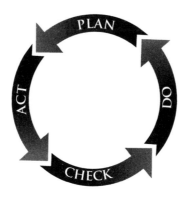

PLAN

The first step, planning, is all about recognizing an opportunity and planning a change. Let's say part of your TQL is beginning an exercise program. You've recognized an opportunity for growth and you need to plan its implementation. You'll have to ask yourself several questions to complete the plan:

1. What do I like to do?
2. What activity will be most beneficial to my health?
3. Have I had a physical in which my doctor has approved of my participation in this type of exercise?
4. If my doctor didn't approve my chosen activity, what are my alternatives?
5. How much time do I have available each day?
6. What time of day is best for my schedule?
7. How many days per week will I be exercising?
8. Do I have the proper equipment? If not, when and where will I get it?

More questions could be asked, but you get the idea: You have to plan your life change, not simply dive into it.

Do

Continuing with the example of beginning an exercise program, let's say you've answered all the questions above and have your doctor's approval to walk three miles, five days a week before work. You've bought your gear, and you're ready to go. On your first day, everything goes great. You jump out of bed and into your clothes you laid out last night and head outside to follow the route you drove earlier to make sure you would walk exactly three miles.

On your second day, you're a bit sore, so you cut your route short and walk only two miles. On day three, it's raining when you wake up, so you roll over, telling yourself you'll make it up on Saturday. Day four is one for

The greatest danger for most of us is not that our aim is too high and we miss it, but that it is too low and we reach it.

—Michelangelo

the books. The weather's great, you feel rested, and three miles fly by. On day five, you hit the snooze alarm. You stayed up late preparing for this morning's meeting, and there's just no way you can drag yourself out of bed. You eventually make it outside, but again, you complete only two miles.

You have a plan, and you are doing it. Now you need to diagnose how well the plan is working. That brings us to the next step.

CHECK

After completing a short *Do* phase, it's time to review the results and identify any changes you need to make.

1. You planned to walk a total of fifteen miles but only completed ten.
2. You were sore on day two.
3. The weather played a major factor in your ability (or initiative) to exercise.
4. Your time management skills affect your ability (or initiative) to exercise.
5. Even though you didn't meet your goal, you accomplished more this week than you did last week.

Having reviewed your initial progress, you're ready to alter your plan to make it more effective.

ACT

Based on your observations from the *Check* phase, you have several choices.

1. You can reduce the number of miles or the number of days you plan to walk.
2. You can consider replacing your shoes and/or socks to help alleviate the soreness you experienced.
3. Since weather can be an obstacle, you can consider purchasing a treadmill or a gym membership.
4. You can set up another PDCA cycle to evaluate your time management skills.
5. You can reward yourself for the steps you took toward living a TQL.

You can, of course, choose a negative route, beating yourself up for not meeting your goal, for being lazy, for mismanaging your time, but those have no place in a TQL. Don't waste your time on them, but if you find yourself drifting toward the negative, review the section on befriending yourself and settle back on the positive as quickly as possible.

Once you've made the necessary adaptations of the *Act* phase, the cycle starts again. By the way, PDCA is a great activity for your journal. It's that simple—and that effective.

TAKE CHARGE OF YOUR LIFE

Essential to a TQL is your understanding that your personal life is your responsibility. I saw a sign in an office recently that read "Your mother doesn't work here. Clean up after yourself." What's true in that office is true in every other facet of your life. Nobody's going to ask if you brushed and flossed this morning, if you balanced your checkbook last week, or if you kissed your spouse before you went to sleep last night. A thousand details in your personal life clamor for your attention, and waiting until your dentist gives you the lecture for not flossing, your bank sends the letter notifying you of multiple overdrafts, and your spouse gives you *the look* for not being affectionate is no way to prioritize. You must take control of your own life.

When I was growing up, my mother used to remind me that it takes less than two minutes to make a bed. Many personal

THE RIGHT ATTITUDE: HELEN KELLER

At less than two years old, Helen Keller came down with a fever that left her blind and deaf. Her remarkable journey to learn to read Braille and communicate through the persistence of her teacher, Anne Sullivan, is dramatized in the play and three movie adaptations called *The Miracle Worker*. Equally miraculous was her ability to live independently for thirty-two years after Sullivan's death.

Keller attributed her remarkable achievements (as someone who could neither hear or see) to her positive attitude. She wrote, "When one door of happiness closes, another opens; but often we look so long at the closed door that we do not see the one which has opened for us."

details take that amount of time or less. But how to determine which ones matter most?

First, start with those that affect your most important relationships. If your spouse appreciates a goodnight kiss, give one. If your daughter needs you to call the school, pick up the phone.

Second, move to your personal habits that affect your secondary relationships—work, church, and social relationships. Keep your voice down when you're on the phone in your cube. Straighten your desk before you leave in the evening. RSVP when it's requested. Be on time.

First say to yourself what you would be; and then do what you have to do.

—Epictetus

Third, consider habits that affect your health. Quit smoking. If you want to keep your teeth, flossing isn't such a bad idea, either. Have a glass of water instead of a soda every day.

Fourth, take care of your finances. I remember being shocked when I realized no bank, mortgage broker, or credit card company cared whether I was in debt. If I wanted to be debt free, I had to begin to work toward that goal.

Finally, focus on what brings order to your life. Make your bed, pick up after yourself (that will go a long way toward building your relationship with your spouse, too), and review the helps on dealing with clutter in chapter 7. When your environment is chaotic, your life tends to be chaotic. When your surroundings are orderly, your life tends to be more peaceful.

MAXIMIZE YOUR SKILLS USE

One of the self-change management techniques you must master is maximizing the use of your own skills. To achieve a TQL, you must major on your strengths rather than focusing on your weaknesses. Here's an example.

Jean was a retired office worker now active in her church and community. I'll never forget the day she said, "I have someone come to clean my house every other week. My gifts and skills aren't all that domestic, so I'd rather spend my time doing what I do well and leave the housework to someone who does that well." My first reaction was one of indignation. *Who does she think she is? She doesn't work full time; she doesn't have kids at home. How dirty can her house get? Surely she has time to clean it! That's an irresponsible use of her family's money.*

Upon further and more rational reflection, however, I realized how courageous and wise her decision was. She knew she risked being judged by mentioning her arrangement, but she also wanted to plant a seed of consideration in my mind. Jean was committed to inspiring and encouraging mothers of young children. She knew she was gifted in that area, and she knew she had something to teach them. She also knew she wouldn't be able to use her gifts if she stayed home and cleaned all day. She and her husband had discussed the idea, and they agreed it was financially feasible. Jean was freed to do what she did best.

Teresa, on the other hand, delights in caring for her home, cooking lovely meals, and entertaining. She believes a clean, orderly home and nutritious meals are a gift she gives her family and others. She uses her skills and talents in ways that serve others and fulfill her.

Now review your skills utilization. Are you doing what you're skilled and gifted to do? If not, why not? Do you need to delegate like Jean did? Do you need to consider a vocational change? If you don't believe you're using your skills the way you need to, apply the PDCA process to make changes.

PRACTICE ACCOUNTABILITY

You may become distracted from the hard work of making life changes—not because you are lazy or unmotivated, but simply because life is demanding. Other things will cause you to lose focus. Accountability is a way to help us from straying too far from our objectives. Knowing we have to answer to someone for our actions can sometimes make the difference between a good and a bad choice. These simple steps will place you under accountability and help ensure that you will be successful in making the life changes you dream of.

And so, dear brothers and sisters who belong to God and are partners with those called to heaven, think carefully about this Jesus whom we declare to be God's messenger and High Priest (Heb. 3:1 NLT).

FIND A PARTNER

Finding an accountability partner can be the most difficult part of this process because you must find the right person for the task. Your spouse automatically qualifies because of your intimate relationship, but sometimes our spouses let us off the hook too easily in order to avoid conflict and being perceived as a nag. Here are some qualities to look for in an accountability partner:

- *Same Gender.* Opposite-sex accountability is a disaster waiting to happen; it never, ever works.
- *Peer Status.* A mentor is different than an accountability partner. Your accountability partner should be relatively equal to you in most ways.
- *Sensitivity and Kindness.* You will want someone who will listen to your struggles without judging.
- *Humility and Wisdom.* A great accountability partner knows when to speak and when to be silent.
- *Transparency.* The ideal accountability partner will be willing to confess his or her own shortcomings. One-sided accountability is a priest or confessor relationship, not a partnership.
- *Trustworthiness.* You must know your partner will keep what's said private.
- *Competency.* Your accountability partner should model the traits to which you aspire. You're not looking for perfection, but your accountability partner should be someone you admire on some level.[9]

ESTABLISH A FORMAT

When you have pinpointed an accountability partner, it will be up to the two of you to decide how often, how long, and where to meet. Allow enough time for both of you to talk, and don't make your meetings so far apart that you forget what's happened in between them. Being face-to-face with your accountability partner is helpful, but you can practice accountability by telephone or e-mail.

SET AN AGENDA

Determining what you'll discuss in your meetings depends on what you want to be held accountable for. If you and your partner are mainly concerned about health issues, then you won't likely be talking about work. Here are three categories under which you can frame specific questions:

- *Goals*—short- or long-term written goals.
- *Follow-Up Items*—events or issues related to a goal or what you previously discussed.
- *General Issues*—family, marriage, work, health, or other issues that have come up since your previous meeting.[10]

Having an accountability partner can help you meet your goals faster, stay focused on what's important in your life, and help you mature as an individual. This will accelerate the pace of your life change and speed you toward the goal of a Total Quality Life.

STEER THE COURSE OF YOUR LIFE

By now you're certain you want to make some changes in life—maybe many changes. You know you need to tweak your eating and exercise habits, you'd like to work on that clutter issue, and you're thinking journaling sounds like something you want to pursue. There are so many options, how can you determine which one or ones to focus on first?

Stephen Covey's second habit of highly effective people is "Begin with the end in mind." Before you start trying to make life changes, you need to know where you're headed. Covey invites his readers to participate in a helpful visualization exercise. In your mind's eye, see yourself going to the funeral of a loved one. Picture yourself driving to the funeral parlor or chapel, parking the car, and getting out. As you walk inside the building, you notice the flowers, the soft organ music. You see the faces of friends and family you pass along the way. You feel the shared sorrow of losing, and the joy of having known, that radiates from the hearts of the people there.

> *I know the price of success: dedication, hard work, and an unremitting devotion to the things you want to see happen.*
>
> —Frank Lloyd Wright

As you walk down to the front of the room and look inside the casket, you suddenly come face to face with yourself. This is your funeral, three years from today. All these people have come to honor you, to express feelings of love and appreciation for your life.

As you take a seat and wait for the services to begin, you look at the program in your hand. There are to be four speakers. The first is from your family. Immediate and extended family—children, brothers, sisters, nephews, nieces, aunts, uncles, cousins, and grandparents—have come from all over the country to attend. The second speaker is one of your friends, someone who can give a sense of what you were as a person. The third speaker is from your work or profession. The fourth is from your church or a community organization where you've been involved in service.

Now think about what you would like each of these speakers to say about you and your life. What kind of husband, wife, father, or mother would you like their words to reflect? What kind of son or daughter or cousin? What kind of friend? What kind of working associate?

But the Lord said to Samuel, "Do not consider his appearance or his height, for I have rejected him. The Lord does not look at the things man looks at. Man looks at the outward appearance, but the Lord looks at the heart"
(1 Sam. 16:7).

What character would you like them to have seen in you? What contributions, what achievements would you want them to remember? Look carefully at the people around you. What difference would you like to have made in their lives?[11]

Take time to consider how you'd respond to Covey's exercise. When you know the answers to the questions he posed, you're ready to map the changes you will need to make in order to achieve that end. That will begin with the creation of a personal mission statement.

CREATE A MISSION STATEMENT

There are many books that treat this subject, so we won't go into great detail on personal mission statements here. In short, your mission statement should include a declaration of your values and what you hope to accomplish in life. Its phrasing and length are up to you. This will be the guiding vision for your TQL. Once you have a mission statement, you can set goals that match the destination you've chosen for yourself.

Set Goals

Setting goals will help clarify and crystallize your mission. You know where you want to end up; now it's time to figure out how to get there. Goal setting is a process, so start by setting life goals. Consider these categories:

- *Art.* Do you want to achieve any artistic goals? If so, what?
- *Attitude.* Is any part of your mindset holding you back? Is there any part of the way you behave that upsets you? If so, set a goal to improve your behavior or find a solution to the problem.
- *Career.* What level do you want to reach in your career?
- *Education.* Is there any knowledge you want to acquire? What information and skills will you need to achieve other goals?
- *Family.* Do you want to be a parent? If so, how are you going to be a good parent? How do you want to be seen by a partner or by members of your extended family?
- *Finances.* How much do you want to earn by what stage?
- *Health.* Are there any athletic goals you want to achieve, or do you want good health deep into old age? What steps are you going to take to achieve this?
- *Pleasure.* How do you want to enjoy yourself?
- *Public Service.* Do you want to make the world a better place by your existence? If so, how?[12]

Once you know your broad-stroke goals, break them down into ten-, five-, three-, and one-year goals. From there, slice them further into monthly, weekly, and daily goals. Simply saying you want to be a certified public accountant won't make it happen. But if you know you want to be a CPA in five years, you know what classes you have to sign up for next Tuesday.

Last, make all your goals SMART: Specific, Measurable, Attainable, Relevant, and Time-bound, and you'll see them realized sooner than you ever imagined.

YOU CAN!

Perhaps the most intimidating thing about making life changes—even those you're eager to make—is the knowledge that you have already tried and failed. You've sworn to lose weight before. You've tried to quit smoking. You made a vow to get out of debt, but you quickly went back on it. It's likely that you've already attempted to make changes in each of the critical areas of your life—and failed. Now you wonder if you will ever make progress at becoming the person you really want to be.

You can, and you will!

TQL is not a magic formula, neither is it a Herculean feat that only a few can achieve. Total Quality Life is for everyone—it is for you! Banish negative thinking from your mind. Set reasonable, measurable goals. Make yourself accountable to others, and reinforce your plans by journaling and creating healthy relationships. You *will* experience life change. You will experience the Total Quality Life.

STEPS TO TOTAL QUALITY

Take these five actions to solidify your resolve to pursue TQL.

1. Identify your greatest source of anger or discouragement. Find a TQL partner with whom you can share these feelings and receive encouragement.

2. If you have not already done so, begin a TQL journal and record your journey toward the Total Quality Life.

3. Choose one of the Befriend Yourself activities and one of the Befriend Others activities listed in this chapter and begin to practice them.

4. Write a mission statement for your life.

5. Within the next thirty days, establish an accountability relationship as described in this chapter and have your first accountability session.

9

ACHIEVEMENT

―――⟡―――

MOVING UP TO A
NEW LEVEL OF LIVING

The Total Quality Life is within your reach.
It will be your reward for purposeful,
disciplined effort.

Gregory the Grub knew there had to be more. Sure, he loved living in the squishy mud at the bottom of the pond, but he just had a feeling he was missing something. He and his friend, Pete, talked about it.

"I can't shake off the feeling that this isn't all there is," said Gregory.

"Of course this is all there is," said Pete. "This is life. What more do you want?"

"Yeah."

"You got the pond and hills and valleys and forests of seaweed and a life to live and a pond to conquer."

"Yeah."

"And your good works to leave to posture, er, posterior."

"Posterity."

"Yeah."

But no matter how hard Pete tried to convince him, Gregory just wasn't satisfied.

One day he said to Pete, "I feel itchy, Pete. I gotta go now."

"Wait!" said Pete, but Gregory was gone.

For reasons he didn't quite understand, Gregory found himself climbing a bulrush toward the surface of the pond. He stuck his head out and immediately got woozy, and his back—it felt as though his back were splitting open. He turned his aching head to look and saw . . . wings! He had wings! And a body with all the colors of the rainbow! He looked around at the blue sky, the shimmering water, and the pink lilies. A whole new world! Gregory had discovered a whole new world.[1]

You, too, are about to discover a whole new world. You now have a mission statement and a collection of goals (written in your journal, I trust) that have the potential to get you where you want to go in life. The only thing remaining is to implement your vision, to act on your dream. A new way of living awaits you. Are you ready to achieve it? Three important ingredients comprise the final steps in your transformation.

DEVELOP A PERSONAL GROWTH PLAN

The first of three remaining items needed for your TQL is a personal growth plan that will provide the resources you need to fulfill your mission and goals.

Start by prioritizing your goals. If your family is suffering because of poor financial decisions, perhaps getting out of debt is at the top of your list. If you've identified a clear career path, maybe working toward a promotion is number two. If your pants are getting a bit snug, maybe a fitness goal needs to be number three, and so on.

> *The quality of a person's life is in direct proportion to their [sic] commitment to excellence, regardless of their chosen field of endeavor.*
>
> —Vince Lombardi

Next, consider five new habits you'll form related to your goals. Back to our example, if getting out of debt is your first goal, then tracking your spending, balancing your checkbook, or using debit cards instead of credit cards may be the habit you want to form. Attaching one new habit to each of your top five goals will be simpler than trying to establish five new habits related to one goal. If one of your goals is fitness related, it's pretty tough to focus on getting up earlier, drinking more water, working out every day, eating a salad for lunch every day, and cutting down sugar and fat all at once. Matching one habit to each goal, however, should be manageable.

Once you've prioritized your goals and identified habits you want to create, determine which resources will help you succeed. Again, pick one resource for each goal-habit combination. For example, if your goal is to get out of debt and you want to establish the habit of tracking your spending, you might choose to read Dave Ramsey's *Total Money Makeover* or Matt Schonefeld's *Abundant Living*. Filling your mind with sound advice, affirmation, and stories from those who've

THE WILL TO BELIEVE: ABRAHAM

Abraham, who is revered by Christians, Jews, and Muslims alike, is a giant of faith. One stellar act of faith was his stubborn confidence that God would give a son to him, in spite of the fact that Abraham and his wife, Sarah, had been childless into their old age.

Sure enough, when Abraham was about one hundred years old, his son Isaac was born. Some time later God directed Abraham to sacrifice that son on an altar. Although God halted the exercise before any sacrifice was made, Abraham demonstrated that he was willing to trust God even though it meant losing the son he'd waited for so long.

That's faith!

already traveled the road you're starting down will further illuminate the path and help you find your way more easily.

PRACTICE GIVING LIVING

The second remaining element in achieving your goal is to practice *giving living*. Having put together your mission, goals, habits, and resources, it would be easy to become self-focused. After all, achieving a TQL is an intense undertaking. You have books to read. Goals to accomplish. People need to step aside and get out of your way. But self-focus is what we need to avoid. That's what *giving living* is for—it takes our eyes off ourselves and keeps our attention directed toward others. Without diminishing your goals and habits, consider implementing one or more of these other opportunities to reach beyond yourself and serve others.

Avoid Being Wasteful

When we focus only on our own needs, it is easy to become wasteful. Opportunities to avoid waste are everywhere. Here are a few ideas for cultivating the habit of personal responsibility and maturity.

- Walk instead of drive.
- Turn off the water while you brush your teeth.
- Maximize your minutes (see chapter 7).
- Shop at a thrifty clothing store.
- Re-heel your shoes.
- Turn off lights.
- Turn down the heat.
- Eat at home.
- Make your own coffee.

You get the idea. Minimize rather than maximize your use of resources. You'll have a lower impact on the planet and a more positive impact upon others.

Champion a Worthy Cause

Is there a cause near to your heart? Get involved in it. Consider your gifts and available time before you sign up to help. If you work full time, fostering homeless animals probably isn't the best way for you to help your local animal shelter. Writing articles for their newsletter or participating in fundraising campaigns might work better for you. Find a good thing that needs to be done—and do it.

Send a Note of Appreciation

Being confident of this, that he who began a good work in you will carry it on to completion until the day of Christ Jesus (Phil. 1:6).

There's no way to go wrong with sending a note of appreciation. For example, if you're a supervisor, pick a different person on your team each day until you've made it through the entire list. Take ten minutes to write and deliver a note that tells one character trait you admire and one action you appreciate. You'll lift your team, create loyalty, and set a positive example.

Visit Someone in the Hospital

Assuming you're not a pastor or chaplain, visiting someone who's in the hospital might be a bit uncomfortable at first. If so, don't worry. As a friend once said to me, "Uncomfortable isn't bad; it's just uncomfortable!" Your time will mean much to the person you visit, and your chances for success will increase greatly if you'll remember these simple guidelines:

- Make the visit brief.
- Quietly offer a prayer.
- Never discuss your own aches and pains.
- Always bring comfort and cheer.

Volunteer in the Community

The options for volunteering are nearly limitless, and volunteering offers several benefits. You can:

- Make important networking contacts.
- Learn or develop skills.
- Gain work experience.
- Build self-esteem and self-confidence.
- Improve health.
- Meet new people.
- Feel needed and valued.
- Make a difference in someone's life.
- Express gratitude for help you may have received in the past from an organization.[2]

Giving living is not a distraction from pursuing the self-transformation that will bring about Total Quality Life. Giving living is the essence of TQL. Focusing on others ensures that your life will remain balanced and under control. You'll be a better person for it.

SAIL ON! SIR FRANCIS DRAKE

When Francis Drake launched his five-ship armada from Plymouth, England, in 1577 to confront the Spanish on the west coast of South America, he had little idea what to expect. For the most part, he was in uncharted waters.

One of the ships had to be abandoned on the east coast of South America. In sailing south for the Straits of Magellan, a strong storm took him off course nearly to the coast of Antarctica, making his the first ships to sail that far south. Once to the Pacific, another violent storm destroyed a second ship and caused a third to return to England.

Despite these setbacks, Scott eventually captured several Spanish ships and returned safely to England. He achieved because he persevered.

LIVE A FIVE-STAR LIFE

The third and last ingredient to achieving success in your quest for change is to embrace the concept I call the *Five-Star Life*. These five character traits will put legs on all your planning and goal setting and make your TQL worth living.

EFFORT

Expending effort doesn't necessarily guarantee success, but not expending effort guarantees failure. Remember, "If it's to be, it's up to me."

ENTHUSIASM

The seven dwarfs and Mary Poppins both had it right—whistling a tune while you work and downing a spoonful of sugar when you're done go a long way to generating enthusiasm, even when the task isn't particularly enjoyable. You have opportunities no one else will ever have. You have opportunities you haven't even imagined yet. You can generate some excitement and enthusiasm for what lies ahead, can't you? Come on! It'll be an adventure!

ENCOURAGEMENT

Don't forget to encourage others along the way. When we change, those closest to us may be forced to change too. The old ways of relating and behaving won't work anymore. Your loved ones and colleagues might become resentful and fearful when this happens. They're not sure how they feel about the new you, and they don't remember signing up to make changes in their lives. Encourage those people who are affected by the new you. Remind them you love and appreciate them the way they are, but applaud any changes they decide to make.

EFFECTIVENESS

Improving your life takes a tremendous amount of work. So, make the work count. If you're beginning an exercise program and you decide to try a stair-climbing machine, learn how to use it appropriately. People who jump on and drape themselves over the side rails aren't getting the most out of their workouts. They're not being effective. Likewise, if one of your goals is to become financially free, reread

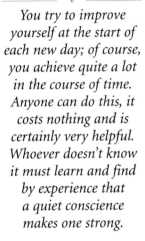

You try to improve yourself at the start of each new day; of course, you achieve quite a lot in the course of time. Anyone can do this, it costs nothing and is certainly very helpful. Whoever doesn't know it must learn and find by experience that a quiet conscience makes one strong.

—Anne Frank

the section about which bills you should pay off first.

EXCELLENCE

Whatever goal or mission you pursue, do so with excellence. You don't have to be the best at something; you just have to be *your* best at it. My friend Mary—the one who finished the Chicago Marathon—took more than six hours to complete the race. The world-record holder ran the race in one-third of that time. But that didn't matter to Mary. She gave that race her best effort—and she has a finisher's medal to prove it. Don't compare yourself to others. Instead, set appropriate standards of excellence, and then meet those standards.

JUST AROUND THE CORNER

You're ready. Your journey toward a TQL is about to begin. With effort, enthusiasm, encouragement, effectiveness, and excellence, I have no doubt you will succeed at what you set yourself to accomplish. I believe you can do it. Stephen Covey wrote, "The best way to predict the future is to create it."[3] You have the information to transform your life, and you have the tools to do it.

Your future starts now.

STEPS TO TOTAL QUALITY

Take these five actions to solidify your resolve to pursue TQL.

1. Create a personal growth plan using the model in this chapter.
2. If you do not currently recycle household items, begin doing so this month. If you do recycle, determine whether there are any items you can reuse rather than disposing of or recycling them.
3. Identify a need that you can meet within your community through volunteerism. Take an action to begin meeting that need this week.
4. Take a Five-Star audit using the points listed in this chapter. Identify which points of the Five-Star Life you will need to embrace or strengthen in order to achieve total quality.
5. Review your progress so far in achieving TQL. Identify areas that you may need to reassess or begin again. Make a revised plan for doing so.

APPENDIX

───────── ✳ ─────────

RESOURCES FOR
TOTAL QUALITY LIVING

DISCIPLINES

With Unveiled Faces: Experience Intimacy with God through Spiritual Disciplines by Keith Drury

Celebration of Discipline by Richard Foster

Six Disciplines for Excellence by Gary Harpst

The Spirit of the Disciplines by Dallas Willard

DIET AND EXERCISE

Minute Motivators for Dieters by Stan Toler

Body for Life by Bill Phillips

Dr. Dean Ornish's Program for Reversing Heart Disease by Dr. Dean Ornish

Eat More, Weigh Less by Dr. Dean Ornish

God's Diet by Dorothy Gault-McNemee

The Ultimate New York Body Plan by David Kirsch

FINANCES

The New Master Your Money by Ron Blue

The Total Money Makeover by Dave Ramsey

Abundant Living by Matt Schonefeld

GIVING

The Cycle of Victorious Giving by Stan and Linda Toler

LEGACY

A Leader's Legacy by Barry Posner

Living Beyond Your Lifetime by Mike Huckabee

Unlocking Your Legacy by Paul Meyer

Mission Statements

The Path: Creating Your Mission Statement for Work and for Life by Laurie Beth Jones

Organization

Getting Organized by Chris Crouch
Organizing Plain and Simple by Donna Smallin

Prayer

The Rhythm of Prayer by Mark A. Moore
Take the Name of Jesus with You by Judy Garlow Wade
Hearing God: Developing a Conversational Relationship with God by Dallas Willard
Prayer: Finding the Heart's True Home by Richard Foster
How to Pray by Elmer L. Towns

Quality Living

The Dream Cycle: Leveraging the Power of Personal Growth by Steve Moore
A Passionate Life by Mike Breen and Walt Kallestad
The Seven Habits of Highly Effective People by Stephen R. Covey
The Secret Blend by Stan Toler

Stress Management

Stress Free for Good by Dr. Fred Luskin and Dr. Kenneth Pelletier
Stress Less by Don Colbert
God's Never Failed Me, but He's Sure Scared Me to Death a Few Times by Stan Toler

Time Management

Stewardship of Time by Stan Toler
Time Management by Harvard Business School Press
The 25 Best Time Management Tools and Techniques by Pamela Dodd and Doug Sundheim

NOTES

CHAPTER 2

1. National Center for Chronic Disease Prevention and Health Promotion, "How Does CDC Measure Population Health-related Quality of Life?" http://www.cdc.gov/hrqol/methods.htm, accessed October 11, 2006.

2. Ibid.

3. Ibid.

4. Economist Intelligence Unit, "The World Leader in Global Business Intelligence," http://www.eiu.com/, accessed November 11, 2006.

5. Economist Intelligence Unit, "The Economist Intelligence Unit's Quality-of-life Index," http://www.economist.com/media/pdf/QUALITY _OF_LIFE.pdf#search='Quality%20of%20Life, accessed November 11, 2006.

6. Usability Net, "International Standards for HCI and Usability" http://www.usabilitynet.org/tools/r_international.htm, accessed November 15, 2006.

7. Wikipedia, "Quality" http://en.wikipedia.org/wiki/Quality, accessed November 11, 2006.

8. Wikipedia, "Guild" http://en.wikipedia.org/wki/Guild, accessed November 11, 2006.

9. W. Edwards Deming's 1950 Lecture to Japanese Management (http://deming.eng.clemson.edu/pub/den/deming_1950.htm). Translated by Teruhide Haga. Accessed June 16, 2006.

10. PBS, *The Deming of America* Petty Consulting/Productions 1991, documentary broadcast on the PBS network.

11. Wikipedia, "W. Edwards Deming," http://en.wikipedia.org/wiki/W._Edwards_Deming, accessed November 11, 2006.

12. Because the name of the International Organization for Standardization would have different abbreviations in different languages (IOS in English, OIN in French), it was decided to use a language-independent word derived from the Greek isos, meaning "equal." Therefore the short form of the organization's name is always ISO. People often ask if we recommend a pronunciation of ISO. Our recommendation is to pronounce it in whichever way comes most naturally. So, you can pronounce it "EZO," "EYE-ZOH" or "EYE-ESS-OH." We don't have any problem with that.

(http://www.iso.org/iso/en/networking/pr/isoname/isoname.html).

13. Wikipedia, "Total Quality Management,"
http://en.wikipedia.org/qiki/Total_Quality_Management, accessed
November 11, 2006.

14. Jack Campanella, "Cost of Quality," http://www.asq.org/learn-about-
quality/cost-of-quality/overview/overview.html, excerpted from the ASQ
Quality Costs Committee, Jack Campanella, ed., *Principles of Quality
Costs: Principles, Implementation, and Use*, 3rd ed. (Milwaukee: ASQ
Quality Press, 1999), 3–5.

15. Wikipedia, "Wallace Carothers,"
http://en.wikipedia.org/wiki/Wallace_Carothers, accessed November 15,
2006.

16. Wikipedia, "Samuel F. B. Morse,"
http://en.wikipedia.org/wiki/Samuel_F._B._Morse, accessed November
17, 2006.

17. "Mother Teresa," http://en.wikipedia.org/wiki/Mother_Teresa,
accessed November 18, 2006.

18. Eternal Word Television Network, "A Vocation of Service,"
http://www.ewtn.com/motherteresa/vocation.htm, accessed November 18,
2006.

19. Mother Teresa, "Her Words,"
http://www.ewtn.com/motherteresa/words.htm, accessed November 18,
2006.

20. Ellen Manila, "57 Cents,"
http://springnotebook.blogspot.com/2006/02/57-centsthe-congregation-
hall-of-grace.html, accessed November 18, 2006.

CHAPTER 3

1. John Piper, "Thoughts on Jesus' Demand to Repent," OnePlace.com,
http://www.oneplace.com/Articles/Print-Friendly.asp?
article_id=1249, accessed May 14, 2007.

2. *Super Size Me*, DVD, directed by Morgan Spurlock (2004, New
York: Hart Sharp Video).

3. David Kleeman, "The Good Things about Television,"
http://www.media-
awareness.ca/english/parents/telvision/good_things_tv.cfm, accessed
November 21, 2006.

4. Karen Jaffe, "Tips for Picking Good TV Shows," http://fun.family
education.com/television/parenting/35759.html, accessed November 21, 2006.

CHAPTER 4

1. Marian Burros, "U.S. Diet Guide Puts Emphasis on Weight Loss,"
New York Times, Jan. 13, 2005,
http://www.nytimes.com/2005/01/13/health/13diet.html?ex=1263358800&

en=1f8721a5eaf6b8f8&ei=5088&partner=rssnyt, and Benjamin Radford, "Fat and Happy: Why Most People Don't Diet" *Skeptical Inquirer*, March 2, 2006, http://www.livescience.com/humanbiology/ 060302_diet_reality.html, accessed November 7, 2006.

2. Pamela Cekola, R.D., and Ruchi Mathur, M.D., "Comparing Popular Weight Loss Diets," http://www.medicinenet.com/script/main/art.asp?articlekey=62965, accessed November 7, 2006.

3. U.S. Food and Drug Administration, "The Facts about Weight Loss Products and Programs," http://www.cfsan.fda.gov/~dms/wgtloss.html, accessed November 7, 2006.

4. Dorothy Gault-McNemee, *God's Diet* (New York: Random, 1999), 13.

5. Mike Breen and Walt Kallestad, *A Passionate Life* (Colorado Springs: Cook, 2005), 61–62.

6. Simone Kelly, "Get a Life, Why Don't Ya!" http://www.adminezine.com/work_and_life_balance.htm, accessed November 7, 2006.

7. Breen and Kallestad, 69.

8. Edward McAuley, et al., "Cardiovascular fitness and neurocognitive function in older adults: a brief review," *Brain Behavior Immunology*, vol. 18, May 2004, 214–20.

9. Alisha L. Brosse, Erin S. Sheets, et al., "Exercise and the Treatment of Clinical Depression in Adults: Recent Findings and Future Directions," *Sports Medicine*, vol. 32, 2002, 741–60.

10. Eugenia Calle and Carmen Rodgriguez, "Overweight, obesity, and mortality from cancer in a prospectively studied cohort of U.S. adults," *New England Journal of Medicine*, vol. 348, April 24, 2003, 1625–38.

11. W. D. Schmidt, C. J. Biwer, et al., "Effects of long versus short bout exercise on fitness and weight loss in overweight females," *Journal of the American College of Nutrition*, vol. 20, October 2001, 494–501.

12. Miriam Nelson and Sarah Wenick, *Strong Women Stay Young* (New York: Bantam, 2000), 12.

13. Successful Aging, "Stress Management Module: Stress-Related Conditions," http://www.successfulaging.ca/programs/stress/09.html, accessed October 8, 2006.

14. Successful Aging, "Stress Management Module: More Practical Suggestions," http://www.successfulaging.ca/programs/stress/26.html, accessed October 8, 2006.

CHAPTER 5

1. M.W. Hodges, "America's Total Debt Report," http://mwhodges.home.att.net/nat-debt/debt-nat-a.htm#household, accessed October 9, 2006.

2. http://www.abiworld.org/ContentManagement/ContentDisplay.cfm?ContentID=18753, accessed October 9, 2006.

3. Kim Khan, "How Does Your Debt Compare?" http://moneycentral.msn.com/content/savinganddebt/p70741.asp, accessed October 9, 2006.

4. Ibid.

5. Creditcards.com, "Credit Card Industry Facts and Personal Debt Statistics," http://www.creditcards.com/statistics/statistics.php, "Credit Card Industry" accessed October 9, 2006.

6. Ibid.

7. Ibid.

8. Ibid.

9. Ibid.

10. For a more detailed discussion of this concept, see my book *The Cycle of Victorious Giving*, published by Beacon Hill Press of Kansas City, 2004.

11. David Bach, *The Automatic Millionaire* (New York: Broadway, 2004), 214.

12. Stan and Linda Toler, *The Cycle of Victorious Giving* (Kansas City: Beacon Hill, 2004), 25–26.

13. Garden Web, http://forums.gardenweb.com/forums/load/tomato/msg1022052022092.html, accessed October 10, 2006.

14. Multilingual Multiscript Plant Name Database, http://www.plantnames.unimelb.edu.au/Sorting/Flageolet.html, "ID Card of the Flageolet Bean," Michael M. Porcher, 1998. Accessed October 10, 2006.

15. Wikipedia, "Jack Benny," http://en.wikipedia.org/wiki/Jack_Benny, accessed October 10, 2006.

16. Earl and Hazel Lee, *The Cycle of Victorious Living* (Kansas City: Beacon Hill, 1995), 39.

17. A. W. Tozer, *The Root of the Righteous* (Christian Publications, 1986).

18. Toler, *Victorious Giving,* 48–49.

19. James 1:17.

20. Toler, *Victorious Giving,* 50.

CHAPTER 6

1. L. Frank Baum, *The Wonderful Wizard of Oz* (New York: Dover, 1960), 58–61.

2. The Teal Trust, "What Is Prayer?" http://prayerguide.org.uk/whatisprayer.htm, accessed November 19, 2006.

3. ACF Newsource, "Gratitude Theory," http://www.acfnewsource.org/religion/gratitude_theory.html, accessed November 19, 2006.

4. Gregg Easterbrook, "Rx for Life: Gratitude," http://www.beliefnet.com/story/51/story_5111_1.html, accessed November 19, 2006.

5. Brother David Stiendl-Rast, "Awake, Aware, and Alert,"

http://www.beliefnet.com/story/79/story_7994_1.html, accessed
November 19, 2006.

6. Holistic-online, "Welcome To The Meditation Infocenter in
HolisticOnline.com!"
http://1stholistic.com/Meditation/hol_meditation.htm, accessed November
19, 2006.

7. Holistic-online, "Types of Meditation—Classification,"
http://1stholistic.com/Meditation/hol_meditation_classification.htm#Conc
entrative, accessed November 19, 2006.

8. Ibid.

9. "Pascal's Wager," http://en.wikipedia.org/wiki/Pascal%27s_Wager,
accessed November 19, 2006.

CHAPTER 7

1. *Merriam-Webster's Collegiate Dictionary*, 11th ed. (Springfield,
MA.: Merriam-Webster, Inc., 2003), 356.

2. Wikipedia, "Value (personal and cultural),"
http://en.wikipedia.org/wiki/Value_(personal_and_cultural), accessed
November 18, 2006.

3. Roy Posner, "The Power of Personal Values,"
http://gurusoftware.com/Gurunet/Personal/Topics/Values.htm, accessed
November 18, 2006.

4. C. Roberts, "Checklist for Personal Values," http://www.selfcounseling.
com/help/personalsuccess/personalvalues.html, accessed November 18,
2006.

5. Help Guide, "Humor and Laughter,"
http://www.helpguide.org/life/humor_laughter_health.htm, accessed
November 18, 2006.

6. Ibid.

7. Discovery Health, "Science of Laughter" quoted in "Humor and
Laughter," http://www.helpguide.org/life/humor_laughter_health.htm,
accessed November 18, 2006.

8. Content provided by OnlineOrganizing.com, offering "a world of
organizing solutions!" Visit www.onlineorganizing.com for organizing
products, free tips, a speakers' bureau, a referral for a professional organizer near you, or help starting and running your own organizing business.

9. Proverbs 22:7, NASB.

10. Jean Chatzky, "The Chatzky Program,"
http://money.cnn.com/2004/09/28/pf/debt/chatzky_program_0404/index.ht
m, accessed November 19, 2006.

11. Chuck Stecker, *Men of Honor, Women of Virtue* (Colorado Springs:
Cook, 2006), 191–92.

CHAPTER 8

1. Amano Books, "Journaling tips," http://www.amanobooks.com/tips/index.html, accessed November 20, 2006.

2. Genesis 2:18.

3. "People," music by Jule Styne, lyrics by Bob Merrill (Columbia Records, 1964).

4. Dean Ornish, M.D., "Love and Survival," http://www.webmd.com/content/article/81/97068.htm, accessed November 18, 2006.

5. Louise Hay, "How to Love Yourself," http://www.seamless-web.net/howto.htm, accessed November 20, 2006.

6. C. Rainfield, "Tips for How to Love Yourself," http://www.kalimunro.com/tips_self-love.html, accessed November 20, 2006.

7. Proverbs 18:24 NKJV.

8. American Society for Quality, "Plan-Do-Check-Act Cycle," http://www.asq.org/learn-about-quality/problem-solving/overview/overview.html, accessed October 18, 2006.

9. Rob Jackson, "How to Develop Effective Accountability," http://www.pureintimacy.org/gr/intimacy/redemption/a0000151.cfm, accessed November 21, 2006.

10. Tom Pryor, "Accountability Part 2," http://www.icms.net/news-44.htm, accessed November 21, 2006.

11. Stephen R. Covey, *The Seven Habits of Highly Effective People* (New York: Simon and Schuster, 1989), 96–97.

12. Mind Tools, "Personal Goal Setting," http://www.mindtools.com/page6.html, accessed November 20, 2006.

CHAPTER 9

1. "Gregory the Grub," told by Ethel Barrett a master storyteller now deceased, is no longer available new. CD's made from the original recordings are available at: www.homeschoolhowtos.com.

2. Canada Volunteerism Initiative, "What Are the Benefits of Volunteering?" http://www.volunteer.ca/volcan/eng/iwant/benefits.php?display=1,3,2, accessed November 21, 2006.

3. Stephen R. Covey, "Keys to Total Quality," http://www.franklincovey.com/fc/library_and_resources/article_library/total_quality/keys_to_total_quality, accessed November 1, 2006.